FUNNY HA-HA, FUNNY PECULIAR
a book of strange & comic poems

This lively anthology brings together two kinds of funny: humorous poems that make you laugh or smile (funny ha-ha), and strange, surreal, witty or plain *weird* poems (funny peculiar). There has always been a tradition of comic and curious verse in English poetry, but in contemporary poetry the peculiar has *really* come into its own, as this surprising selection shows, with poems on:

1 ● **The Opposite Sex:** Love, desire, romance, sex, men & women, adultery & celibacy.

2 ● **Matters of Life & Death:** Life, growing up, growing old, bums & hips, swearing & shaving, amnesia & the end.

3 ● **Nowt So Funny as Folk:** Shops & wheelbarrows, poets & artists, jobs and jobless, war & oppression.

4 ● **Peculiar Places:** Skunks in America, England & Scotland, curries & selfies, Armageddon & colonic irrigation.

5 ● **Sounds True:** Lies & beliefs, Popes & poodles, fire alarms, tennis, rain, static, and Country & Western music.

6 ● **Animal Magic:** Goats, sheep, chickens, yaks, cows, bison, horses, herons, chameleons & crustaceans. And people…

7 ● **Words &** Worse: Adages & proverbs, curses & clichés, slang & swearing. An…

Neil Astley is editor of Bloodaxe Books, which he founded in 1978. His many books include novels, poetry collections and anthologies, most notably the Bloodaxe *Staying Alive* trilogy: *Staying Alive* (2002), *Being Alive* (2004) and *Being Human* (2011).

He has published two comic novels, *The End of My Tether* (2002), which was shortlisted for the Whitbread First Novel Award, and *The Sheep Who Changed the World* (2005). In 2012 Candlestick Press published his selection of *Ten Poems About Sheep* in its renowned pamphlet series.

He lives in Tarset, Northumberland, where there are more sheep than people.

FUNNY HA-HA, FUNNY PECULIAR

a book of strange & comic poems

edited by
NEIL ASTLEY

BLOODAXE BOOKS

ISBN: 978 1 85224 961 8

First published 2015 by
Bloodaxe Books Ltd,
Eastburn,
South Park,
Hexham,
Northumberland NE46 1BS.

www.bloodaxebooks.com
For further information about Bloodaxe titles
please visit our website or write to
the above address for a catalogue.

Supported using public funding by
**ARTS COUNCIL
ENGLAND**

Printed in Great Britain by Bell & Bain Limited, Glasgow, Scotland, on
acid-free paper sourced from mills with FSC chain of custody certification.

Contents

3 ● NOWT SO FUNNY AS FOLK

1 ● THE OPPOSITE SEX

A Declaration of Need

JOHN HEGLEY

I need you like a novel needs a plot.
I need you like the greedy need a lot.
I need you like a hovel needs a certain level of grottiness
to qualify.
I need you like acne cream needs spottiness.
Like a calendar needs a week.
Like a colander needs a leek.
Like people need to seek out what life on Mars is.
Like hospitals need vases.
I need you.
I need you like a zoo needs a giraffe.
I need you like a psycho needs a path.
I need you like King Arthur needed a table
that was more than just a table for one.
I need you like a kiwi needs a fruit.
I need you like a wee wee needs a route out of the body.
I need you like Noddy needed little ears,
just for the contrast.
I need you like bone needs marrow.
I need you like straight needs narrow.
I need you like the broadest bean needs something else on the plate
before it can participate
in what you might describe as a decent meal.
I need you like a cappuccino needs froth.
I need you like a candle needs a moth
if it's going to burn its wings off.

Choice

CONNIE BENSLEY

You're the one I boned up mah jongg for
You're the one I bought the chaise longue for
You're the one I yearn to go wrong for.

You're the one I'll garden my plot with
You're the one I'll throw in my lot with
You're the one I'll find my G spot with.

You're the one I've had my teeth capped for
You're the one my scruples were scrapped for
You're the one I get all unwrapped for:
                    You're the one.

Love poem

GREGORY O'BRIEN

Houses are likened to shoeboxes but shoeboxes are not
likened to houses. A car is likened to a heap but a heap is not
likened to a car. A child is a terror but terror is not a child.
A business might be a sinking ship but a sinking ship is no
business. A bedroom is a dog's breakfast but a dog's breakfast
is not a bedroom. A bad review might be a raspberry but a
raspberry is not a bad review. A haircut is likened to a disaster
but a disaster is not a haircut. Books can be turkeys but turkeys
are never books. A holiday might be a riot but a riot is not a
holiday. A garden might become a headache but a headache is
not a garden. I dream about you but you are not a dream.

The Did-You-Come-Yets of the Western World

RITA ANN HIGGINS

When he says to you:
You look so beautiful
you smell so nice –
how I've missed you –
and did you come yet?

It means nothing,
and he is smaller
than a mouse's fart.

Don't listen to him…
Go to Annaghdown Pier
with your father's rod.
Don't necessarily hold out
for the biggest one;
oftentimes the biggest ones
are the smallest in the end.

Bring them all home,
but not together.
One by one is the trick;
avoid red herrings and scandal.

Maybe you could take two
on the shortest day of the year.
Time is the cheater here
not you, so don't worry.

Many will bite the usual bait;
they will talk their slippery way
through fine clothes and expensive perfume,
fishing up your independence.

These are
the did-you-come-yets of the western world,
the feather and fin rufflers.
Pity for them they have no wisdom.

Others will bite at any bait.
Maggot, suspender, or dead worm.
Throw them to the sharks.

In time one will crawl
out from under thigh-land.
Although drowning he will say,
'Woman I am terrified, why is this house
shaking?'

And you'll know he's the one.

You Don't Know What Love Is

KIM ADDONIZIO

but you know how to raise it in me
like a dead girl winched up from a river. How to
wash off the sludge, the stench of our past.
How to start clean. This love even sits up
and blinks; amazed, she takes a few shaky steps.
Any day now she'll try to eat solid food. She'll want
to get into a fast car, one low to the ground, and drive
to some cinderblock shithole in the desert
where she can drink and get sick and then
dance in nothing but her underwear. You know
where she's headed, you know she'll wake up
with an ache she can't locate and no money
and a terrible thirst. So to hell
with your warm hands sliding inside my shirt
and your tongue down my throat
like an oxygen tube. Cover me
in black plastic. Let the mourners through.

Please Can I Have a Man

SELIMA HILL

Please can I have a man who wears corduroy.
Please can I have a man
who knows the names of 100 different roses;
who doesn't mind my absent-minded rabbits
wandering in and out
as if they own the place,
who makes me creamy curries from fresh lemon-grass,
who walks like Belmondo in *A Bout de Souffle*;
who sticks all my carefully-selected postcards –
sent from exotic cities
he doesn't expect to come with me to,
but would if I asked, which I will do –
with nobody else's, up on his bedroom wall,
starting with Ivy, the Famous Diving Pig,
whose picture, in action, I bought ten copies of;
who talks like Belmondo too, with lips as smooth
and tightly-packed as chocolate-coated
(*melting* chocolate) peony buds;
who knows that piling himself stubbornly on top of me
like a duvet stuffed with library books and shopping-bags
is all too easy: please can I have a man
who is not prepared to do that.
Who is not prepared to say I'm 'pretty' either.
Who, when I come trotting in from the bathroom
like a squealing freshly-scrubbed piglet
that likes nothing better than a binge
of being affectionate and undisciplined and uncomplicated,
opens his arms like a trough for me to dive into.

Romantic Moment

TONY HOAGLAND

After seeing the documentary we walk down Canyon Road,
onto the plaza of art galleries and high end clothing stores

where the mock orange trees are fragrant in the summer night
And the smooth adobe walls glow fleshlike in the dark.

It is just our second date, and we sit down on a bench,
holding hands, not looking at each other,

and if I were a bull penguin right now I would lean over
and vomit softly into the mouth of my beloved

and if I were a peacock I'd flex my gluteal muscles to
erect and spread the quills of my Cinemax tail.

If she were a female walkingstick bug she might
insert her hypodermic probiscus delicately into my neck

and inject me with a rich hormonal sedative
before attaching her egg sac to my thoracic undercarriage,

and if I were a young chimpanzee I would break off a nearby tree limb
and smash all the windows in the plaza jewelry stores.

And if she was a Brazilian leopardfrog she would wrap her impressive
tongue three times around my right thigh and

pummel me lightly against the surface of our pond
and I would know her feelings were sincere.

Instead we sit awhile in silence, until
she remarks that in the relative context of tortoises and iguanas,

human males seem to be actually rather expressive
And I say that female crocodiles really don't receive

enough credit for their gentleness.
Then she suggests that it is time for us to go

do something personal, hidden, and human.

Three Sisters

IVOR CUTLER

The only place my boyfriend
will make love to me is
on the cinder path that leads
up to the outside lavy.
I lie on my bare bum
in the moonlight
on the cold cinders
assuaging his needs
my back hair in mud
and my heels in a puddle.
I wear stout clothes then
never my best.
My mother and father never
go to the lavatory whilst
we are at our loving
so
we have the path to ourselves.
My big sister gets it in
the vegetables and my little
sister against the back door.
What a family we are!

One Minute with Eileen

DERMOT HEALY

1

After finishing work
I take a shortcut through Soho

and pass an open door
that says: two pounds

for one minute with Eileen
Well, I ponder this,

then turn and turn about.
The old lady behind the counter

gives me a blue ticket.
Sit there, she says, Eileen

is occupied at present.
I'll wait on the street, I say

2

So I took a turn or two
through the Chinese,

like a man about
business in the town,

and soon enough, a youth
doused in gel emerges

head-down
like a duck in thunder

and high-tailed it
in a north-easterly,

and the lady waved me in.
The inside door opened and

I sit in an armchair
facing Eileen.

   3
Now, she explains,
I'm a tipsy girl.

If you want to touch me,
that's twenty; if you want me

to touch you, that's forty.
Full sex is sixty.

Anything after that
is over a hundred.

And what, I asked,
do I get for my two pound?

You get to hear the prices, she said.

For sixpence

IVOR CUTLER

For a sixpence
I whisper,
'You are beautiful.'
For a shilling
I whisper,
'You are beautiful,
despite certain unfortunate features.'
For a florin
I call
'What an
interesting physiognomy
you possess.'
For five bob,
'You are
exceedingly ugly.'
For ten,
'Ech!'
And,
for a quid,
'I love you!'

Kipper
on the Lips

PETER FINCH

O Cod,
I feel a right prawn.
Try to kipper outside the cinema.
Obviously the wrong plaice.
Welcoming bream turns into a foul mackerel,
next minnow she's slapping my face.
I'm amazed.
What a dolphin to do.
Have I got halibutosis? A stickle back?
Squid in my trousers? No way.
I'm just a flash haddock after her turbots.
Look at this conger eel, I say.
But she's into big bivalves
and long-distance gurnards,
so I flounder,
What a elver time to distrust
your encrustation.
The sea trout's out, I'm a failure.
She goes off with a sperm whale.
I light up a bloater.

Forecasting

JULIA DARLING

He was a viking in his forties.
Tyne after tyne I said, don't dogger me,
just don't dogger me – but he fishered,
me a single parent with no german bite.

I came to like his humber,
and eventually thames towards him.
Dover and dover
we caught the white of each other's lundy,
throwing all faroes into the fast net,
deep in our irish sea,
rockallin' and dancin' the malin.
Those were the hebrides years.
Until Cromarty.

How I wish Cromarty had not met my viking.

Still only forty, we tyned and doggered,
until my fisher ran out.
And he got his german bite all right,
humbering halfway up the Thames,
waves dover him,
his white in the dark lundy,
faroes swept from the fast net.

I have drunk the Irish Sea,
hearing him, calling through ships,

Rockall – Malin – CROMARTY!

Thanks Cromarty. I hope you sink,
someday.

Trouble Came to the Turnip

CAROLINE BIRD

When trouble came to the village,
I put my love in the cabbage-cart
and we rode, wrapped in cabbage,
to the capital.

When trouble came to the capital,
I put my love in the sewage pipe,
and we swam, wrapped in sewage,
to the sea.

When trouble came to the sea,
I put my love inside a fish
and we flitted, wrapped in fish,
to the island.

When trouble came to the island,
I put my love on a pirate ship
and we squirmed, wrapped in pirate,
to the nunnery.

When trouble came to the nunnery,
I put my love inside a prayer book
and we repented, wrapped in prayer,
to the prison.

When trouble came to the prison,
I put my love on a spoon
and we balanced, wrapped in mirror,
to the soup.

When trouble came to the soup,
I put my love inside a stranger
and we gritted, wrapped in mouth
to the madhouse.

When trouble came to the madhouse,
I put my love on a feather
and we flapped, wrapped in feather,
to the fair.

When trouble came to the fair,
I put my love inside a rat,
and we plagued, wrapped in rat,
to the village.

When trouble came to the village,
I put my love in the turnip-lorry
and we sneaked, wrapped in turnip,
a hurried kiss.

Stanley

LORRAINE MARINER

Yesterday evening I finished
with my imaginary boyfriend.
He knew what I was going to say
before I said it which was top of my list
of reasons why we should end it.

My other reasons were as follows:
he always does exactly what I tell him;
nothing in our relationship has ever surprised me;
he has no second name.

He took it very well
all things considered.
He told me I was to think of him
as a friend and if I ever need him
I know where he is.

My Inner Bloke

JOANNE LIMBURG

When I feel like a drag queen
in tights and heels,
I put that down
to my Inner Bloke.

He's the one
who always has to win,
who comes into his own
in seminars and pub debates.

He knows a lot of facts
and loves to swap them.
There's nothing he won't
turn into a joke,

including me.
He's a bully like that
and needs to put me down.
He's a thwarted thug

and it's all thanks to me,
the body he lives through,
my puny little arms,
that girly way I kick.

How She Puts It

GEOFF HATTERSLEY

'It's about time you grew up' she says,
as though he doesn't know that theory.

'All I said' he starts to say
but she's not interested

in all he said, slamming
the door as she leaves.

He's both feet on her coffee table
when she later tells him it's over:

'Get out and take your ugliness with you'
is how she puts it.

Bitcherel

ELEANOR BROWN

You ask what I think of your new acquisition;
and since we are now to be 'friends',
I'll strive to the full to cement my position
with honesty. Dear – it depends.

It depends upon taste, which must not be disputed;
for which of us *does* understand
why some like their furnishings pallid and muted,
their cookery wholesome, but bland?

There isn't a *law* that a face should have features,
it's just that they generally *do*;
God couldn't give colour to *all* of his creatures,
and only gave wit to a few;

I'm sure she has qualities, much underrated,
that compensate amply for this,
along with a charm that is so understated
it's easy for people to miss.

And if there are some who choose clothing to flatter
what beauties they think they possess,
when what's underneath has no shape, does it matter
if there is no shape to the dress?

It's not that I think she is *boring*, precisely,
that isn't the word I would choose;
I know there are men who like girls who talk nicely
and always wear sensible shoes.

It's not that I think she is vapid and silly;
it's not that her voice makes me wince;
but – chilli con carne without any chilli
is only a plateful of mince...

Rubbish at Adultery

SOPHIE HANNAH

Must I give up another night
To hear you whinge and whine
About how terribly grim you feel
And what a dreadful swine
You are? You say you'll never leave
Your wife and children. Fine;

When have I ever asked you to?
I'd settle for a kiss.
Couldn't you, for an hour or so,
Just leave them out of *this*?
A rare ten minutes off from guilty
Diatribes – what bliss.

Yes, I'm aware you're sensitive:
A tortured, wounded soul.
I'm after passion, thrills and fun.
You say fun takes its toll,
So what are we doing here? I fear
We've lost our common goal.

You're rubbish at adultery.
I think you ought to quit.
Trouble is, at fidelity
You're also slightly shit.
Choose one and do it properly
You stupid, stupid git.

Smokers for Celibacy

FLEUR ADCOCK

Some of us are a little tired of hearing that cigarettes kill.
We'd like to warn you about another way of making yourself ill:

we suggest that in view of AIDS, herpes, chlamydia, cystitis and NSU,
not to mention genital warts and cervical cancer and the proven
          connection between the two,

if you want to avoid turning into physical wrecks
what you should give up is not smoking but sex.

We're sorry if you're upset,
but think of the grisly things you might otherwise get.

We can't see much point in avoiding emphysema at sixty-five
if that's an age at which you have conspicuously failed to arrive;

and as for cancer, it is a depressing fact
that at least for women this disease is more likely to occur in the
          reproductive tract.

We could name friends of ours who died that way, if you insist,
but we feel sure you can each provide your own list.

You'll notice we didn't mention syphilis and gonorrhoea;
well, we have now, so don't get the idea

that just because of antibiotics quaint old clap and pox
are not still being generously spread around by men's cocks.

Some of us aren't too keen on the thought of micro-organisms travelling up
        into our brain
and giving us General Paralysis of the Insane.

We're opting out of one-night stands;
we'd rather have a cigarette in our hands.

If it's a choice between two objects of cylindrical shape
we go for the one that is seldom if ever guilty of rape.

Cigarettes just lie there quietly in their packs
waiting until you call on one of them to help you relax.

They aren't moody; they don't go in for sexual harassment and threats,
or worry about their performance as compared with that of other cigarettes,

nor do they keep you awake all night telling you the story of their life,
beginning with their mother and going on until morning about their first wife.

Above all, the residues they leave in your system are thoroughly sterilised
        and clean,
which is more than can be said for the products of the human machine.

Altogether, we've come to the conclusion that sex is a drag.
Just give us a fag.

Doo-wop girls of the universe

FINUALA DOWLING

I know something you don't know
about the women you know –
those makers of decisions,
physicians, rhetoricians,
amiable stage technicians,
indignant politicians,
formidable statisticians,
quiet dieticians
and the non-icians too,
the lovely -ists:
the linguists,
lyricists,
artists,
activists.

Almost every woman I've ever known –
whether she be -ician or she be -ist –
has told me once or shown
she'd really come into her own as
a doo-wop girl.

So put her in the footlights,
put her at the backing mikes,
right up there on the dais,
maybe slightly out of focus
while some man sings his opus,
the undisputed locus
of attention.

Then while the main man
belts out the main track
she'll be in the back
going like so –
shoulders, head and toes –
hips, chest, east, west.
Best way to describe her pose
is 'biding',
she's biding time on the sidelines
waiting for the best lines –
the reprise –
the one we're born cooing:
ooby shooby doo
right on cue.

Look, I'm known to generalise
but I'd like to emphasise
that every woman has inside
a doo-wop girl.

Give her the mike, Mike
or I'll call my sisters,
'cause I got sisters,
and I'll say: 'Sisters,
you hang up those rubber gloves
you freeze that chicken

you unplug that iron
you come with me
we be free
we be threeness
we be supremes
we be the unforced
force of fourness
not sad, not terse:
doo-wop girls of the universe.'

The Old Debate of Don Quixote vs Sancho Panza

PRISCILA UPPAL

The men in this family
are much stupider than the women, my large-armed uncle says.
But the women all go crazy.

They go crazy because they read books.
They write books.
They learn languages and go to artsy movies.

The men like to work, to do.
We are happy walking for hours into the woods to cut down a tree
or transporting boxes from one garage to another.
As long as there is something to carry, an object to touch
and exchange, we feel less alone in this universe and know our place.
We know how to play beach volleyball,
how to fix cars and airplanes,
how to enjoy the sun on our foreheads in the sweltering heat.

The women in this family
are never happy. Always thinking, thinking, thinking
about this and that, that and this,
they know only thoughts running in circles, circles,
until exhausted and dizzy.
The women are too smart for their own good.
The books worm out holes in their brains.

They are unhappy in every language they learn.
And so maybe the men in this family are smarter than we think.

Don't Waste Your Breath

GLYN MAXWELL

On sales or sermons at my door,
Contributions from the floor,
    Screaming things.
Wondering where the good times went,
Complaining to this Government,
    Reciting 'Kings'.

Telling fibs to Sherlock Holmes,
Games of tag with garden gnomes,
    Soliloquies.
Knock-knock jokes on a Croatian,
Great ideas for situation
    Comedies.

Asking her to reconsider
Leaving, trying to kid a kidder,
    Roundelays.
Entering for field events,
Just causes or impediments
    On wedding days.

Begging rides in backs of hearses,
Happy Birthday's other verses,
        Asking twice.
Musing on your point-blank misses,
Moaning 'This is hell' or 'This is
        Paradise.'

Offering a monk your ticket,
Using metaphors from cricket
        When in Texas.
Telephoning during finals,
Remonstrating in urinals
        With your Exes.

Phrases like 'Here's what I think',
Giving up girls/smoking/drink
        At New Year.
Asserting that all men are equal,
Settling down to write a sequel
        To *King Lear*.

Revisions to *The Odyssey*,
Improvements on Psalm 23
        Or hazel eyes.
Glueing back the arms on Venus,
Any other rhyme than 'penis',
        The Turner Prize.

Interrogating diplomats,
Defining Liberal Democrats,
    Begging to banks.
Supporting Malta's football team,
Translating King's 'I have a dream'
    Into the Manx.

Reading verse to lesser mammals,
Tailing cats or humping camels,
    Hectoring sheep.
Pleading with a traffic warden,
Writing things that sound like Auden
    In his sleep.

Don't waste your breath on telling me
My purpose, point or pedigree
    Or wit or worth.
Don't waste your breath explaining how
A poem works, or should do now
    You're on the Earth.

Don't waste your breath on rage, regret
Or ridicule; don't force or fret,
    Breathe easily.
Remember: every starlit suck
Is seven trillion parts good luck
    To one part me.

The Awfulisers

MICHAEL LEUNIG

Every night and every day
The awfulisers work away,
Awfulising public places,
Favourite things and little graces;
Awfulising lovely treasures,
Common joys and simple pleasures;
Awfulising far and near
The parts of life we held so dear:
Democratic, clean and lawful,
Awful, awful, awful, awful.

Well

FINUALA DOWLING

When I am down my well,
the one with slippery black sides,
no tocholes, and only a pinhole
of light 3000 compass turns above,
I still describe myself as 'fine'.

I am thinking of saying 'well'
instead. Yes, I think in future
I will definitely reply, 'I am well'.

'Well' is more accurate,
and more of a cry for help.

Burst Pipe with 'A Level' Notes

IAN McMILLAN

Here I am, carrying   Narrator?
this empty kettle through a clear   Persona?
December night,   Winter of the Soul?

My Dad a few yards behind,   God/Christ?
my wife at home, mopping,   Madonna?
looking at the water   Sense of making whole?

coming through the ceiling.   Virgin birth?
That blinking red eye   Drink?
of the aeroplane   Idea of Heaven?

We see every night at this time   Eternity?
and that girl   Made-up?
with the made-up face   Pun on Fiction?

collecting the Avon   Scavenger?
catalogues. Ding Dong.   Doorbell?
Face framed in the door.   Like a portrait?

Every time I ring   Prayer?
the plumber's mobile phone   Plumber = God?
he doesn't answer it.   Church and state?

When he left our house   Desertion by God?
he said he was going   Looking into darkness?
to look into a loft.   Severed head?

I fill the kettle
at my mother's. She gives
me some bacon.

Family life?
Bacon?
Is God dead?

Spiderweb

KAY RYAN

From other
angles the
fibers look
fragile, but
not from the
spider's, always
hauling coarse
ropes, hitching
lines to the
best posts
possible. It's
heavy work
everyplace,
fighting sag,
winching up
give. It
isn't ever
delicate
to live.

I ran away from home...

MICHAEL ROSEN

I ran away from home. I said, I'm going on the Aldermaston March to ban the bomb. They said that this was out of the question, the boy's mad. Crazy. My mother said, Where will you stay? You'd have nothing to eat, you don't know anyone, what would you eat? You're not going. Harold, say something, he's too young, look at him, he's packing. You can't go without a spare pair of trousers, how can he carry a bag like that for twenty miles a day? Stop him, Harold. What would you do in the evening? You need to eat, you get ill if you don't eat. Take a tin of beans. You can always eat beans. Harold, stop him. There's the chicken. Take the chicken. If you're taking a tin of beans, take two. He's thirteen, Harold. Go next year, wait till next year, they won't have banned the bomb by then, believe me. There'll be another march. Go on that one. You must keep eating fresh fruit. And you like dates. He's always liked dates, hasn't he, Harold? Just squeeze them in down the side of the bag. Couldn't he wait till the last day, when we'll be there? We can all go to Trafalgar Square together. Harold, have you got the chicken? Just because it's Easter, doesn't mean it's warm. It can snow at Easter. Wear the string vest. Who's organised the coaches? Do we know these people, Harold? One orange! Take five. And raisins. He's thirteen. It's ridiculous. He can't go. Keep the chicken wrapped. Phone us if you need more food. Goodbye.

The Voice in which My Mother Read to Me

JONATHAN EDWARDS

isn't her good morning, good afternoon, good night voice,
her karaoke as she dusts, make furniture polite voice,
her saved for neighbours' babies and cooing our dog's name voice.

It isn't her best china, not too forward, not too shy voice,
or her dinner's ready, your room looks like a sty voice,
or her whisper in my ear as she adjusts my tie voice.

It's not her roll in, Friday night, *Lucy in the Sky* voice,
her Sunday morning, smartest frock, twinkle-in-the-eye voice,
that passing gossip of the vicar with the Communion wine voice.

It's not her 'Gateau – no, ice cream – no... I can't make the choice' voice.
It's not her decades late, fourth change, 'Is this skirt smart enough?' voice.
It's not her caught me with the girl from number twenty-one voice.

That voice which she reserved for twelve-foot grannies, Deep South hobos,
that sleepy, secret staircase, selfish giants, Lilliput voice.
That tripping over, 'Boy why is your house so full of books?' voice.

Self-Portrait, Rear View

SHARON OLDS

At first I almost do not believe it, in the hotel
triple mirror, that that is my body, in
back, below the waist, and above
the legs – the thing that doesn't stop moving
when I stop moving.
And it doesn't even look like just one thing,
or even one big, double thing
– even the word saddlebags has
a smooth calfskin feel to it,
compared to this compendium
of net string bags shaking their booty of
cellulite fruits and nuts. Some lumps
look like bonbons translated intact
from chocolate box to buttocks, the curl on top
showing, slightly, through my skin. Once I see what I can
do with this, I do it, high-stepping
to make the rapids of my bottom rush
in ripples like a world wonder. Slowly,
I believe what I am seeing, a 54-year-old
rear end, once a tight end,
high and mighty, almost a chicken butt, now
exhausted, as if tragic. But this is not
an invasion, my cul-de-sac is not being
used to hatch alien cells, ball peens,
gyroscopes, sacks of marbles. It's my hoard
of treasure, my good luck, not to be
dead, yet, though when I flutter
the wings of my ass again, and see,
in a clutch of eggs, each egg

on its own, as if shell-less, shudder, I wonder
if anyone has ever died
looking in a mirror, of horror. I think I will
not even catch a cold from it,
I will go to school to it, to Butt
Boot Camp, to the video store, where I saw,
in the window, my hero, my workout jelly
role model, my apotheosis: *Killer Buns.*

homage to my hips

LUCILLE CLIFTON

these hips are big hips
they need space to
move around in.
they don't fit into little
petty places. these hips
are free hips.
they don't like to be held back.
these hips have never been enslaved,
they go where they want to go
they do what they want to do.
these hips are mighty hips.
these hips are magic hips.
i have known them
to put a spell on a man and
spin him like a top!

My Father's Vocabulary

TONY HOAGLAND

In the history of American speech,
he was born between 'Dirty Commies' and 'Nice tits'.

He worked for Uncle Sam,
and married a dizzy gal from Pittsburgh with a mouth on her.

I was conceived in the decade
between 'Far out' and 'Whatever';

at the precise moment when 'going all the way'
turned into 'getting it on'.

Sometimes, I swear, I can feel the idiom flying around inside
        my head
like moths left over from the Age of Aquarius.

Or I hear myself speak and it feels like I am wearing
a no-longer-groovy cologne from the seventies.

In those days I was always trying to get a rap session going,
and he was always telling me how to clean out the garage.

Our last visit took place in the twilight zone of a clinic,
between 'feeling no pain' and 'catching a buzz'.

For that occasion I had carefully prepared
a suitcase full of small talk

– But he was already packed and going backwards,
with the nice tits and the dirty commies,

to the small town of his vocabulary,
somewhere outside of Pittsburgh.

Shaven Heads

ADRIAN MITCHELL

Men in their twenties with shaven heads
Men in their thirties with shaven heads
Men in their forties with shaven heads
They all look alike to me

Their noses jut out like ruddy rockets
Their eyeballs bulge out of their sockets

They smile all the time at people from foreign parts
To show they are not skinhead racist farts

But that smile too frequently unzips
Like a leer and bald heads speak louder than lips

It must feel so weird when you're shaving your crop
Put that razor away grow some sort of a mop

But don't overdo it or I shall wail
Get out of here with your fuzzy pony-tail

Forgetfulness

BILLY COLLINS

The name of the author is the first to go
followed obediently by the title, the plot,
the heartbreaking conclusion, the entire novel
which suddenly becomes one you have never read, never even
      heard of.

It is as if, one by one, the memories you used to harbor
decided to retire to the southern hemisphere of the brain,
to a little fishing village where there are no phones.

Long ago you kissed the names of the nine Muses goodbye
and watched the quadratic equation pack its bag,
and even now as you memorise the order of the planets,

something else is slipping away, a state flower perhaps,
the address of an uncle, the capital of Paraguay.

Whatever it is you are struggling to remember
it is not poised on the tip of your tongue,
not even lurking in some obscure corner of your spleen.

It has floated away down a dark mythological river
whose name begins with an *L* as far as you can recall,
well on your own way to oblivion where you will join those
who have even forgotten how to swim and how to ride a bicycle.

No wonder you rise in the middle of the night
to look up the date of a famous battle in a book on war.
No wonder the moon in the window seems to have drifted
out of a love poem that you used to know by heart.

The Inability to Recall the Precise Word for Something

*All things are words
of some strange tongue*

JORGE LUIS BORGES

OLI HAZZARD

The first person you see after leaving your house
One who always wants to know what's going on
To make money by any means possible
A surgical sponge accidentally left inside a patient's body
Given to incessant or idiotic laughter
An incestuous desire for one's sister
The act of mentally undressing someone
One who speaks or offers opinions on matters beyond their
        knowledge
A secret meeting of people who are hatching a plot
The act of beating or whipping schoolchildren
The categorisation of something that is useless or trivial
Belching with the taste of undigested meat
One who is addicted to abusive speech
The use of foul or abusive language to relieve stress or ease
        pain
The condition of one who is only amorous when the lights
        are out
To blind by putting a hot copper basin near someone's eyes
The act of opening a bottle with a sabre
The habit of dropping in at mealtimes
The act of killing every twentieth person
One who eats frogs
The low rumbling of distant thunder
Someone who hates practising the piano
The practice of writing on one side of the paper
A horse's attempt to remove its rider
The collective hisses of a disapproving audience
The sensation that someone is mentally undressing you

The act of self-castration
Being likely to make a mistake
One who fakes a smile, as on television
Counting using one's fingers
The act or attitude of lying down
The smell of rain on dry ground
The space between two windows

Samsara

GUS FERGUSON

For over thirty years
I've ridden, I've raced

and, at least once,
replaced

every part,
including the frame,

but nevertheless
it remains the same,

it's still my bike
and still it's whole.

A metaphor, if you like,
for the transcendent human soul.

The Antiques Shop

RUSSELL EDSON

There was a man who wanted to buy an old man in an antiques shop: How much for that old man?

You do me too much honor, but owing to my youth I'm not for sale, smiled the old man who was standing behind a counter of antique bellybuttons.

How much for that piece of biological trash?

One man's trash is sometimes another man's treasure, smiled the old man, who was wearing a bellybutton on his forehead like a third eye.

You're old enough to be dead, said the man, but still young enough to be put on a stick for a scarecrow. So how much are you asking for that old man?

He's not old enough to be sold as an authentic antique, smiled the old man who was now wearing the bellybutton on one of his earlobes.

By the way, what's with that bellybutton?

Oh that, I'm trying to find the right place to grow my new umbilical cord.

But you're too old for an umbilical cord.

I know, smiled the old man, isn't it wonderful...

Let Me Die a Youngman's Death

ROGER McGOUGH

Let me die a youngman's death
not a clean & inbetween
the sheets holywater death
not a famous-last-words
peaceful out of breath death

When I'm 73
& in constant good tumour
may I be mown down at dawn
by a bright red sports car
on my way home
from an allnight party

Or when I'm 91
with silver hair
& sitting in a barber's chair
may rival gangsters
with hamfisted tommyguns burst in
& give me a short back & insides

Or when I'm 104
& banned from the Cavern
may my mistress
catching me in bed with her daughter
& fearing for her son
cut me up into little pieces
and throw away every piece but one

Let me die a youngman's death
not a free from sin tiptoe in
candle wax & waning death
not a curtains drawn by angels borne
'what a nice way to go' death

Not for Me a Youngman's Death

ROGER McGOUGH

Not for me a youngman's death
Not a car crash, whiplash
John Doe at A&E kind of death.
Not a gun in hand, in a far-off land
IED at the roadside death

Not a slow-fade, razor blade
bloodbath in the bath, death
Jump under a train, Kurt Cobain
bullet in the brain, death

Not a horse-riding paragliding
mountain climbing fall, death.
Motorcycle into an old stone wall
you know the kind of death, death

My nights are rarely unruly.
My days of all-night parties
are over, well and truly.

No mistresses no red sports cars
no shady deals no gangland bars
no drugs no fags no rock 'n' roll
Time alone has taken its toll

Let me die an oldman's death
Not a domestic brawl, blood in the hall
knife in the chest, death.
Not a drunken binge, dirty syringe
'What a waste of life' death.

Not a rumour, a murmur

GUS FERGUSON

It starts to beat before you're born
and thumps away from dawn to dawn.

The heart that's trapped inside your chest,
is not allowed to take a rest

and here's a fact both sad and true:
that when it stops, then so do you.

My Funeral

WENDY COPE

I hope I can trust you, friends, not to use our relationship
As an excuse for an unsolicited ego-trip.
I have seen enough of them at funerals and they make me cross.
At this one, though deceased, I aim to be the boss.
If you are asked to talk about me for five minutes, please do not
>> go on for eight.
There is a strict timetable at the crematorium and nobody wants
>> to be late.
If invited to read a poem, just read the bloody poem. If requested
To sing a song, just sing it, as suggested,
And don't say anything. Though I will not be there,
Glancing pointedly at my watch and fixing the speaker with a
>> malevolent stare,
Remember that this was how I always reacted
When I felt that anybody's speech, sermon or poetry reading was
>> becoming too protracted.
Yes, I was impatient and intolerant, and not always polite
And if there aren't many people at my funeral, it will serve me
>> right.

Tullynoe:
Tête-à-Tête
in the Parish
Priest's
Parlour

PAUL DURCAN

'Ah, he was a grand man.'
'He was: he fell out of the train going to Sligo.'
'He did: he thought he was going to the lavatory.'
'He did: in fact he stepped out the rear door of the train.'
'He did: God, he must have got an awful fright.'
'He did: he saw that it wasn't the lavatory at all.'
'He did: he saw that it was the railway tracks going away from him.'
'He did: I wonder if…but he was a grand man.'
'He was: he had the most expensive Toyota you can buy.'
'He had: well, it was only beautiful.'
'It was: he used to have an Audi.'
'He had: as a matter of fact he used to have two Audis.'
'He had: and then he had an Avenger.'
'He had: and then he had a Volvo.'
'He had: in the beginning he had a lot of Volkses.'
'He had: he was a great man for the Volkses.'
'He was: did he once have an Escort?'
'He had not: he had a son a doctor.'
'He had: and he had a Morris Minor too.'
'He had: he had a sister a hairdresser in Kilmallock.'
'He had: he had another sister a hairdresser in Ballybunion.'
'He had: he was put in a coffin which was put in his father's cart.'
'He was: his lady wife sat on top of the coffin driving the donkey.'
'She did: Ah, but he was a grand man.'
'He was: he was a grand man…'
'Good night, Father.'
'Good night, Mary.'

How Sweet the Dead Are Now

**FINUALA
DOWLING**

How sweet the dead are now they've stopped
sleeping around and wanting royalties and fame.

How dear the dead are now that they've given up
drinking so much and opening the door in their underpants.

How unvexing the dead are now that they pay their way
and only come when invited.

Next time you visit, remind me to play you
a few cuts from my boxed set of the dead.

Such a sweet sound, this turning round in graves.

3 ● NOWT SO FUNNY AS FOLK

In Phil's Butchers

GEOFF HATTERSLEY

They're sure they know me from somewhere:
'Aren't tha t' bloke that rode naked
on a bike through Jump for charity?
Thi picture wa' in t' Chronicle.'
The previous customer leaves, coughing
something red and green onto the pavement.
'That's a poorly mister, dead on 'is feet 'e is.'
One of them decides he worked
with my brother at Johnson's
though I've no brother who worked there.
'Are tha sure?' he wonders.
An older man (is it Phil?)
pops his head in from the back room:
'Leave t' lad alone 'n' gi' 'im 'is pies.'
I hold them in my hand as I say 'Ta-ra'
and leave, taking off my dark glasses.
There's a patch of blue sky
where my eyes should be, which startles
an old woman crossing the road.
'By,' I say, to reassure her,
'it's cold enough for a walking stick.'
'All laughter is despair,' she replies,
'it's t' human condition, like.'

The fundament of wonderment

MATTHEW WELTON

She said her name was little jones
and bended back her finger-bones

and sang a song in minor thirds.
She spilled a smile and spoke her words.

*

Up here the river turns its boats.
she brings out books of pencil-notes,

her letters from, her letters to,
her clarkesville park, her london zoo.

*

And, in the wind and where she walks
above the blue nasturtium-stalks

at london zoo, the smells of apes
are like the smells of table-grapes.

*

The mice and monkeys tell the trees
the wind will end, the worlds will freeze.

She moves herself beyond the grass
the blue boats pass. The blue boats pass.

Ten Ways to Avoid Lending Your Wheelbarrow to Anybody

ADRIAN MITCHELL

1 *Patriotic*

May I borrow your wheelbarrow?
I didn't lay down my life in World War II
so that you could borrow my wheelbarrow.

2 *Snobbish*

May I borrow your wheelbarrow?
Unfortunately Samuel Beckett is using it.

3 *Overweening*

May I borrow your wheelbarrow?
It is too mighty a conveyance to be wielded
by any mortal save myself.

4 *Pious*

May I borrow your wheelbarrow?
My wheelbarrow is reserved for religious ceremonies.

5 *Melodramatic*

May I borrow your wheelbarrow?
I would sooner be broken on its wheel
and buried in its barrow.

6 *Pathetic*

May I borrow your wheelbarrow?
I am dying of schizophrenia
and all you can talk about is wheelbarrows.

7 *Defensive*

May I borrow your wheelbarrow?
Do you think I'm made of wheelbarrows?

8 *Sinister*

May I borrow your wheelbarrow?
It is full of blood.

9 *Lecherous*

May I borrow your wheelbarrow?
Only if I can fuck your wife in it.

10 *Philosophical*

May I borrow your wheelbarrow?
What is a wheelbarrow?

The Prince

SAM RIVIERE

let a man sit down I'm in telesales me
would you buy off this voice on a phone
what do they call you Sarah Sarah Sarah
do you find me attractive Sarah
I don't mind if you don't I'm a bit tipsy
I'm celebrating maybe I'll tell you
if we get to know each other better
Sarah you're beautiful you know
never let a man tell you otherwise
right don't be that way nice girls Sarah
who's your friend Melanie where you from
how old are you woo is it true when
I get you home are you going to let me
spank it I'm going to spank it I'm
going to hold that caramel cheek in
my palm I'm coming round soon later
I love you baby you think I can't hear all
that soft boy shit let her know what
you're going to do she don't want you
she wants me she don't want you she
wants me you may as well delete my
number you had your chance today and
blew it it's Geoffrey Geoffrey with a J

Singh Song!

DALJIT NAGRA

I run just one ov my daddy's shops
from 9 o'clock to 9 o'clock
and he vunt me not to hav a break
but ven nobody in, I do di lock –

cos up di stairs is my newly bride
vee share in chapatti
vee share in di chutney
after vee hav made luv
like vee rowing through Putney –

Ven I return vid my pinnie untied
di shoppers always point and cry:
Hey Singh, ver yoo bin?
Yor lemons are limes
yor bananas are plantain,
dis dirty little floor need a little bit of mop
in di worst Indian shop
on di whole Indian road –

Above my head high heel tap di ground
as my vife on di web is playing wid di mouse
ven she netting two cat on her Sikh lover site
she book dem for di meat at di cheese ov her price

my bride
      she effing at my mum
      in all di colours of Punjabi
      den stumble like a drunk
      making fun at my daddy

my bride
　　　tiny eyes ov a gun
　　　and di tummy ov a teddy

my bride
　　　she hav a red crew cut
　　　and she wear a Tartan sari
　　　a donkey jacket and some pumps
　　　on di squeak ov di girls dat are pinching my sweeties –

Ven I return from di tickle ov my bride
di shoppers always point and cry:
Hey Singh, ver yoo bin?
Di milk is out ov date
and di bread is alvays stale,
di tings yoo hav on offer yoo hav never got in stock
in di worst Indian shop
on di whole Indian road –

Late in di midnight hour
ven yoo shoppers are wrap up quiet
ven di precinct is concrete-cool
vee cum down whispering stairs
and sit on my silver stool,
from behind di chocolate bars
vee stare past di half-price window signs
at di beaches ov di UK in di brightey moon –

from di stool each night she say,
　　How much do yoo charge for dat moon baby?

from di stool each night I say,
　　Is half di cost ov yoo baby,

from di stool each night she say,
　　How much does dat come to baby?

from di stool each night I say,
　　Is priceless baby –

A Man Besotted by his Batch

PAUL DURCAN

In the Spar supermarket on Merrion Row,
Opposite O'Donoghue's public house,
When I presented my basket at the checkout
To my dismay it was taken
Not by one of the many Polish girls manning the checkouts
But by a short, stocky, curly, red-headed male Dubliner
Screeching to himself 'The Auld Triangle'
By Brendan Behan:
And the auld triangle
Goes jingle jangle
All along the banks
Of the Royal Canal.

He was all bonhomie but not excessively.
He commented on my every item
But when I handed him
My batch loaf of bread
He seized-up, swooned, swayed, roared:
'Jasus!' he exploded. 'A batch!'
He continued as if performing an aria in the *Messiah*
'When I was in Australia – and don't get me wrong –
I loved it in Australia – every Dublin man
Should spend time in Australia –
But the one thing I missed was my batch.
After seven years in Perth – Jasus!
You should see the women in Perth! –
When I came home to Dublin
The first thing I did was to go out
And buy myself a batch
And I came back with my batch
And I smeared two slices with dollops of butter
And I made one gorgeous ham sandwich.
The women of Perth, O Jasus, forgive me,
But there's nothing – not even a Perth woman –
To beat a batch. Thank you, sir. Have a good day.'

Front Gate

**BRENDAN
KENNELLY**

I met Ace de Horner at the Front Gate
of Trinity College. He was looking out
for Kennelly. 'Why are you looking for him?'
I asked. 'Because the bastard makes me dumb
with anger at times,' said Ace, 'and I'd like
to give him a bloody good piece o' me mind.
I'm in the right mood for that. It's time to strike
a blow.' 'Why bother?' I said, 'sure he's only a fat
bollocks at the best o' times. You'd see him there
arsing like an ape across Front Square,
a big smile on his foolish face.
He used to be a fuckin' disgrace
in the old days, a hoor for the drink,
he'd floor whiskey out of a hole in the road.
As for being an academic, sure the man can't think.
Why did they ever let him in there, in the name o' God?
It used to be a mortal sin to go to Trinity College
without the Archbishop's permission,
but that little fucker is uglier than any mortal sin.'

'I'll tell you this,' said Ace, 'he's a cute Kerry hoor,
he'll go in a swingdoor behind you, and before
you know where you are, he's out in front o' you.
He'd get in where the wind would turn back!
Why don't they give the bastard the sack?'

'What do you think of his poetry?' I asked.

'Bad, black, blasphemous rubbish,' Ace replied,

'published by these Bloodaxe Bastards in Newcastle upon Tyne.
There's one thing sure! They'll never publish mine!'

'They tell me Kennelly was married once,' I said.
'But the drunken bollocks went clean out of his head
and his wife, a decent woman, a fine, tall,
intelligent woman towering head and shoulders over that small
knacker, threw him out. She was too good for him.
Of that there is no doubt.'

'Not only that,' said Ace, 'I hear he's a womanising prick,
he'd ride a cracked saucer in the thick
of a storm, he'd screw a poxy cat
miaowing through a skylight like a wounded
lyricist of the Celtic Twilight, he'd tip
a midge in a mist,
quarter, half or totally pissed.'

'I see,' I said, 'that's helpful to know.
But he's arrogant and vain also.
He's foolish, too, if you know what I mean.
He advertises Toyota cars
and the little bollocks can't even drive!
I mean, did you ever see such crap in your life?
Is there a poet among us with such an under-
developed sense of the ridiculous?
Jesus, it'd make you wonder!'

Ace de Horner stood between the statues
of Oliver Goldsmith and Edmund Burke.

He gestured aloft, right and left, and said
in obvious pain, deeply aesthetic pain:
'To think that such men
came out of Trinity College, and see
what it produces today.
A fucking car-salesman
pretending to be a poet!
Do you know what?
I'm glad I haven't met him!
If I did, I'd cut the balls off him!'

'Mr de Horner,' I said, 'Don't work yourself up.
A major poet like you
should have nothing to do
with a venal wretch like Kennelly.
It's better to calm down and go your way.'

Between Burke and Goldsmith, Ace
stood, statue-like, all passion, honour and grace.
'Yes,' he said, 'yes, how right you are
A true poet must follow his own star
though it lure him
into the damned heart of eternity.
I think I'll walk out to Sandymount strand
and stroll by the buttock loosening sea.
Yes. To ease my soul, that's what I'll do.'

He started to move, halted, turned.

Black Moon

**MATTHEW
SWEENEY**

For white he used toothpaste,
for red, blood – but only his own
that he hijacked just enough of each day.

For green he crushed basil in a little
olive oil. His yellow was egg yolk,
his black, coal dust dampened with water.

He tried several routes to blue
before stopping at the intersection
of bilberry juice and pounded bluebells.

His brown was his own, too, applied
last thing in the day before the first
Laphraoig, and the stone jug of ale.

He used no other colours, but his tone
was praised by Prince Haisal, no less,
which got him a rake of commissions

and a residency-offer in Kuwait
which he turned down. At home
the Royal Family was less generous

so he painted them all, in a series
that came to be called his brown period,
though this was strictly incorrect.

He never exhibited with other painters,
never drank with them, spoke of them –
never even spat at their work.

A cave in the Orkneys was his last dwelling
and he rode a horse to his studio.
There were no people in these paintings,

which were found piled up on one another
inside the cave, with no sign of him,
and on top was a depiction of a black moon.

Pit Closure as Art

IAN McMILLAN

In the centre of
the major retrospective
there is a door
which you open.

As you open it
certain nerves
in the face
are jangled
artificially:
you smile.

The smile becomes
the property of
The Artist.

Beyond the door
is a room
and another door.

You walk over to the door.

The catalogue says
'The door will not be locked'
but the catalogue also
is part of The Art.

The door is locked.
The door you came through
is locked. The Artist
has served The Art well.

As you stand there
certain nerves
in the eyes
are jangled
artificially:
you weep.

The tears become
the property of
The Artist

You dig to keep warm.
The Artist arrests you for digging.
The Artist smashes your head
for pounding on the door.

The Artist prevents you
from walking to the door.

All this is part of The Art.
The Artist has refined The Art well.

You will be hearing from us shortly

U.A. FANTHORPE

You feel adequate to the demands of this position?
What qualities do you feel you
Personally have to offer?

                                        Ah

Let us consider your application form.
Your qualifications, though impressive, are
Not, we must admit, precisely what
We had in mind. Would you care
To defend their relevance?

                                    Indeed

Now your age. Perhaps you feel able
To make your own comment about that,
Too? We are conscious ourselves
Of the need for a candidate with precisely
The right degree of immaturity.

                              So glad we agree

And now a delicate matter: your looks.
You do appreciate this work involves
Contact with the actual public? Might they,
Perhaps, find your appearance
Disturbing?

                                    Quite so

And your accent. That is the way
You have always spoken, is it? What
Of your education? Were
You educated? We mean, of course,
Where were you educated?

And how
Much of a handicap is that to you,
Would you say?

                          Married, children,
We see. The usual dubious
Desire to perpetuate what had better
Not have happened at all. We do not
Ask what domestic disasters shimmer
Behind that vaguely unsuitable address.

And you were born – ?

                                   Yes. Pity.

So glad we agree.

Job Description

DUNCAN FORBES

Dogsbody. Despot. Saint and martyr.
Diplomat. Bureaucrat. Creep and tartar.
Tamer of lions, cobra-charmer.
Nuclear warhead and disarmer.
Expert with parents, sons and daughters,
Weasel words and troubled waters.
Menagerie manager/manageress,
A human dynamo hooked on stress.
An innovative facilitator,
Proactive professional loyalist traitor.
Workaholic with sense of balance,
Renaissance figure with multi-talents,
Gravitas and a winning smile,
Impeccable manners and perfect style.
A drudge, a drone, a worker ant,
A meek impoverished sycophant
Who craves acceptance and admittance,
Suffers fools gladly, works for a pittance.
Name two referees, one of them God.
No weirdos please. Apply in blood.

Women's Inhumanity to Women

(Galway Labour Exchange)

RITA ANN HIGGINS

And in this cage, ladies and gentlemen,
we have the powers that be.

Powder power,
lipstick power,
pencil power,
paper power,
cigarette in the left-hand power,
raised right of centre half-plucked eyebrow,
Cyclops power,
big tits power,
piercing eyes power,
filed witches' nails power,
I own this building power,
I own you power,
fear of the priest power,
fear of the Black 'n' Tans power.

Your father drank too much power,
your sister had a baby when she was fifteen power,
where were you last night power,
upstairs in your house is dirty power,
the state of your hotpress power,
the state of your soul power,
keep door closed power,
keep eyes closed power,
no smoking power,
money for the black babies power,

queue only here power,
sign only there power,
breathe only when I tell you power.

No pissing on the staff power,
jingle of keys power,
your brother signs and works power,
ye have a retarded child power,
you sign and work power,
look over your shoulder power,
look over your brother's shoulder power,
I know your mother's maiden name power,
look at the ground power,
I know your father's maiden name power,
spy in the sky power,
spy in the toilet power,
fart in front of a bishop power.

Apologise for your mother's colour hair power,
apologise for your father's maiden name power,
apologise for being born power.

The Ice Cream Man

JAMES TATE

I answered the ad in the paper. I had been unemployed for nine months and was desperate. At the interview, the man said, 'Do you have much experience climbing tall mountains?' 'Absolutely. I climb them all the time. If I see a tall mountain, I have to climb it immediately,' I said. 'What about swimming long distances in rough ocean waters, perhaps in a storm?' he said. 'I'm like a fish, you can't stop me. I just keep going in all kinds of weather,' I said. 'Could you fly a glider at night and land in a wheat field, possibly under enemy fire?' he said. 'Nothing could come more naturally to me,' I said. 'How are you with explosives? Would a large building, say, twenty stories high present you with much difficulty?' he said. 'Certainly not. I pride myself on a certain expertise,' I said. 'And I take it you are fully acquainted with the latest in rocket launchers and land mines?' he said. 'I even own a few myself for personal use. They're definitely no problem for me,' I said. 'Now, Mr Strafford, or may I call you Stephen, what you'll be doing is driving one of our ice cream trucks, selling ice cream to all the little kids in the neighborhood, but sometimes things get tricky and we like all our drivers to be well-trained and well-equipped to face any eventuality, you know, some fathers can get quite irate if you are out of their kid's favorite flavor or if the kid drops the cone,' he said. 'I understand, I won't hesitate to take appropriate action,' I said. 'And there are certain neighborhoods where you're under advisement to expect the worst, sneak attacks, gang tactics, bodies dropping from trees or rising out of manholes, blockades, machine gun fire, launched explosives, flamethrowers and that kind of thing. You can still do little business there if you are on your toes. Do you see what I'm saying?' he said. 'No problem. I know those kinds of neighborhoods, but, as you say, kids still want their ice cream and I won't let them down,' I said. 'Good, Stephen, I think you're going to like this job. It's exciting and challenging. We've, of course, lost a few drivers over the years, but mostly it was because they weren't paying attention. It's what I call the Santa Claus complex. They thought they were there just to make the kids happy. But there's a lot more to it than that. One of our best drivers had to level half the city once. Of course, that was an extreme case, but he did what needed to be done. We'll count on you to be able to make that kind of decision. You'll have to have all your weapons loaded and ready to go in a moment's notice. You'll have your escape plans with you at all times,' he said 'Yes, sir, I'll be ready at all times,' I said. 'And, as you know, some of the ice cream is lethal, so that will require a quick judgment call on your part as well. Mistakes will inevitably be made, but try to keep them at a minimum, otherwise the front office becomes flooded with paperwork,' he said. 'I can assure you that I will use it only when I deem it absolutely necessary,' I said. 'Well, Stephen, I look forward to your joining our team. They're mostly crack professionals, ex-Green Berets and Navy Seals and that kind of thing. At the end of the day you've made all those kids happy, but you've also thinned out the bad seeds and made our city a safer place to be,' he said. He sat there smiling with immense pride. 'How will I know which flavor is lethal?' I said. 'Experiment,' he said. I looked stunned, then we both started laughing.

Managing the Common Herd

(two approaches for senior management)

JULIE O'CALLAGHAN

THEORY X: People are naturally lazy.
They come late, leave early, feign illness.
When they sit at their desks
it's ten to one they're yakking to colleagues
on the subject of who qualifies as a gorgeous hunk.
They're coating their lips and nails with slop,
a magazine open to 'What your nails say about you'
or 'Ten exercises to keep your bottom in top form'
under this year's annual report.
These people need punishment;
they require stern warnings
and threats – don't be a coward,
don't be intimidated by a batting eyelash.
Stand firm: a few tears, a Mars Bar,
several glasses of cider with her pals tonight
and you'll be just the same old
rat-bag, mealy-mouthed, small-minded tyrant
you were before you docked her
fifteen minutes pay for insubordination.

Never let these con-artists get the better of you.

THEORY Z: Staff need encouragement.
Give them a little responsibility
and watch their eager faces lighting up.
Let them know their input is important.
Be democratic – allow all of them
their two cents worth of gripes.
(Don't forget this is the Dr Spock generation.)

If eight out of twelve of them
prefer green garbage cans to black ones
under their desks, be generous –
the dividends in productivity
will be reaped with compound interest.
Offer incentives, show them
it's to their *own* advantage to meet targets.
Don't talk down to your employees.
Make staff believe that they
have valid and innovative ideas
and that not only are you interested,
but that you will act upon them.

Remember, they're human too.

Fight Song

DEBORAH GARRISON

Sometimes you have to say it:
Fuck them all.

Yes fuck them all –
the artsy posers,
the office blowhards
and brown-nosers;

Fuck the type who gets the job done
and the type who stands on principle

the down-to-earth and understated;
the overhyped and underrated;

Project director?
Get a bullshit detector.

Client's mum?
Up your bum.

You can't be nice to everyone.

When your back is to the wall
When they don't return your call
When you're sick of saving face
When you're screwed in any case

Fuck culture scanners, contest winners,
subtle thinkers and the hacks who offend them;
people who give catered dinners
and (saddest of sinners) the sheep who attend them –

which is to say fuck yourself
and the person you were: polite and mature,
a trooper for good. The beauty is
they'll soon forget you

and if they don't
they probably should.

Ruling-Class Sonnet with Capitals and Obscenities

JOHN WHITWORTH

Bad people are out there, extremely bad
And into some extremely scary stuff,
Unreasonable people, BLOODY MAD
DOGS to be frank; you have to treat them rough.
Their purpose is to overthrow the state.
Democracy is not the thing at all
And utmost rigour is appropriate
Countering forces so inimical.
Fill out the enclosed therefore, in triplicate
With photographs, two for each and one for luck
Attested by a Justice of the Peace,
Vicar, solicitor or, WHAT THE FUCK,
Some nob, then send it back to the Police.
NONE OF US NEEDS TO TAKE THIS SORT OF SHIT.

The enemy out there, that evil axis,
Is plotting, as we speak, to terrorise
Your families, and double all your taxes,
Unless you take the steps that we advise.
FILL OUT THIS FUCKING FORM. It's clear enough.
Complete the twenty-seven sections, sign
And send it back tout de suite. We need this stuff.
For why? WE SWEAT FOR YOU LIKE SODDING SWINE.
From dawn to dusk, and this is all the thanks
We get. SWEET JESUS, we're the government;
You *voted* for us once. Just check the blanks.
And tick the box. Our people represent
Your only hope just when you need it most.
Believe it, Sunshine, OR YOU'RE BLEEDING TOAST.

This Be
The Worst

BENJAMIN ZEPHANIAH

They fuck you up, those lords and priests.
    They really mean to, and they do.
They fill themselves at highbrow feasts
    And only leave the crumbs for you.

But they were fucked up long ago
    By tyrants who wore silly gowns,
Who made up what they didn't know
    And gave the masses hand-me-downs.

The rich give misery to the poor.
    It deepens as they hoard their wealth.
They'll be fucked up for ever more,
    So just start thinking for yourself.

Plague Victims
Catapulted over
Walls into
Besieged City

THOMAS LUX

Early germ
warfare. The dead
hurled this way turn like wheels
in the sky. Look: there goes
Larry the Shoemaker, barefoot, over the wall,
and Mary Sausage Stuffer, see how she flies,
and the Hatter twins, both at once, soar
over the parapet, little Tommy's elbow bent
as if in a salute,
and his sister, Mathilde, she follows him,
arms outstretched, through the air,
just as she did on earth.

The People
of the Other
Village

THOMAS LUX

hate the people of this village
and would nail our hats
to our heads for refusing in their presence to remove them
or staple our hands to our foreheads
for refusing to salute them
if we did not hurt them first: mail them packages of rats,
mix their flour at night with broken glass.
We do this, they do that.
They peel the larynx from one of our brothers' throats.
We de-vein one of their sisters.
The quicksand pits they built were good.
Our amputation teams were better.
We trained some birds to steal their wheat.
They sent to us exploding ambassadors of peace.
They do this, we do that.
We canceled our sheep imports.
They no longer bought our blankets.
We mocked their greatest poet
and when that had no effect
we parodied the way they dance
which did cause pain, so they, in turn, said our God
was leprous, hairless.
We do this, they do that.
Ten thousand (10,000) years, ten thousand
(10,000) brutal, beautiful years.

I See a Lily on Thy Brow

DEAN YOUNG

It is 1816 and you gash your hand unloading
a crate of geese, but if you keep working
you'll be able to buy a bucket of beer
with your potatoes. You're probably 14 although

no one knows for sure and the whore you sometimes
sleep with could be your younger sister
and when your hand throbs to twice its size
turning the fingernails green, she knots

a poultice of mustard and turkey grease
but the next morning, you wake to a yellow
world and stumble through the London streets
until your head implodes like a suffocated

fire stuffing your nose with rancid smoke.
Somehow you're removed to Guy's Infirmary.
It's Tuesday. The surgeon will demonstrate
on Wednesday and you're the demonstration.

Five guzzles of brandy then they hoist you
into the theater, into the trapped drone
and humid scuffle, the throng of students
a single body staked with a thousand peering

bulbs and the doctor begins to saw. Of course
you'll die in a week, suppurating on a camphor-
soaked sheet but now you scream and scream,
plash in a red river, in sulfuric steam

but above you, the assistant holding you down,
trying to fix you with sad, electric eyes
is John Keats.

The Native Americans

JAMES TATE

'We found them on your lawn this morning, about seventy-five of them,' the officer said. 'What are they?' I said. 'Well, they're some kind of Native Americans, we don't know what kind yet, but we will. We used an electrical device to paralyse them, but they'll start coming to in about twenty-four hours. Some of them will only live for about an hour, and others could live as long as sixty years. So we'll start in reeducating them right away,' he said. 'But where did they come from?' I said. 'Well, we don't really know, but some of our scientists think they just rose up out of the ground, some signal goes off in them, like a timer,' he said. 'You mean all this time I have been living in a cemetery?' I said. 'Apparently,' he said. 'Well, that explains a lot,' I said. 'What do you mean?' he said. 'Just recently I have felt the house shake a lot at night, and I thought I heard distant cries, and I would wake covered in sweat, which I thought was blood,' I said. 'Why don't you come down here tomorrow morning and we'll show you some of the men,' he said. 'Thank you, Officer,' I said. Of course I was made miserable by the thought that these men had been buried beneath my lawn all these years, but what could I do? The lawn was an unholy mess. It would have to be completely redone in the spring. I showed up at the police department around 10:00 the next morning as told. There behind glass doors were these half-awake men, moaning and shuffling about. 'They don't look very dangerous,' I said to the officer. 'That's why I wanted you to come in early. I didn't want you to see that part of it,' he said. 'What do you do then?' I said. 'More electricity. Then slowly we start to reeducate. Some of them will go quite far,' he said. 'And what about the others?' I said. 'Oh, we'll rebury them with a jolt that will keep them down a good long time,' he said. 'In my yard?' I said. 'That's their native ground,' he said.

Nursery Rhyme

SIMON RAE

Little Bo Peep has lost her sheep
And doesn't know where to find them

Their heads are off and in the trough
With their hoofs laid out beside them

Intestinal tracts are bagged in sacks
With the rest of the offal to bind them

While Farmer Jones has taken the bones
Off to his farm to grind them

Into the schlock he will feed his stock
With their tails falling off behind them.

America

DUNCAN FORBES

We changed the tyre, we changed the wheel,
approached the thing with vim and zeal,
we bathed the parts in motor oil,
we took the auto to the wash
and sprayed it with a pressure hose,
we tried denial, tried to josh,
oh shit, we said, but shit smelt better
than this excremental foetor.
We went berserk with lemon juice,
we tried to turn the demon loose
and exorcise its stinking ghost.
Grease monkeys underneath the chassis
from Frisco Bay to Tallahassee,
we tried the lot from fruit to louche,
from ketchup to vaginal douche,
in car parks right across the States,
detergents, sprays and sublimates,
deodorants, deodorisers,
atom bombs and atomisers,
but could we rid it of the rank
offending stench of reeking skunk?
We learnt to dread the vehicle
as if it owned the pungent smell,
as if the murder was our meal
and we were in a kind of hell.

The car keys and upholstery
began to stink of yesterday.
A creature walking in the road
had heard its skin and bone explode
and in its death throes it had squirted
skunk-spray at the thing which hurt it.
The car became a coffin where
we decomposed and breathed the air.

The Good Ship Venus

JOHN HARTLEY WILLIAMS

Don't lean on the cenotaph unless you can spell it
You haven't packed the hydrangeas with the Gatling gun, I hope?
Too many bruises flew out of the opened grave & began to vaseline
      the moonstones
Trigger-desolation, I call it, but the Queen had her dogs out again
You cd feel that England was being reduced to an air mistress by
      the nephews of royal jelly
Bees were conspiring to fossilise laundries
Oranges, born of skull onions, were being released into the oil
You can see how England attracts dryads in T-shirts
Even tho there are no T-shirts worth wearing in Leicestershire
England prefers the heartening presence of diaries to bolts of
      lightning

The soul of a nation which is being drowned by novelists can only open the
        coffin of its knickers to the sly
So let us keep diaries
They can survive on babies, fish & chips & mosquitoes, if they have to
And when the diaries have astronomical fits in public
Show them mice glue

Mice glue! Mice glue!
England sinks to its knees like a giraffe with no legs
Its keepers tenderly bring it morsels of piranha fish, wrapped in dentifrice leaves
Will it have children in captivity?
I don't think so
You can't run before you can listen to mortgage relief
England becomes ethereal
England varnishes Michaelmas with tunics
I can't hold on very long to this brainstorm of sealion televisions

I feel like a man who has been defenestrated by an unlubricated periscope

I feel like having a beer

Cheerio

Our Ends in the North

KATE FOX

On the first day the world ended,
I said 'Least said soonest mended.
Sometimes these things are sent to try us.'
Though in this case, they were sent to fry us.
But in the North we don't like to make a fuss us,
though sometimes, I admit, we make a bit of a fuss
about how we don't make a fuss.
In fact that 'No Fuss Festival'
with the new play by Alan Bennett
Not Fussed
and the 38-act opera *Unfussy*
starring Lesley 'I Never Make a Fuss Me' Garrett
might, upon reflection
have constituted making a fuss.
But just because it's Doomsday, there's no need to make
a big song and dance about it.
On the second day I was on the bus
when there was a bang and all the lights went out –
and there was a chorus,
of 'Call this an Apocalypse? I felt nowt'.
and 'Grimsby hasn't looked this good since
the Germans redecorated'.
You've got to make the best of things,
Northerners are tough like that
nobody else compares.
On the third day, the Tyne Bridge fell into a crack
in the space-time continuum
I said, 'I'll go to the foot of our stairs,'
but when I got home, there weren't any.

On the fourth day,
Cleckheaton exploded.
I said, 'Worse things happen at sea,'
and popped on a Bear Grylls DVD.
On the fifth day the government said it was tough for everyone,
with it being the Apocalypse
but that actually in London the restaurants were full
and maybe we just weren't trying hard enough
in Liverpool, Newcastle and Hull.
We should get on our bikes
and there not being any roads left, or bikes, was just an excuse.
On the sixth day, the streets were full of people
wandering about, moaning.
The Zombies hadn't come –
it was just folk complaining about the price of petrol
and how the Co-op had run out of white sliced.
On the seventh day Greggs' Ham and Armageddon pasties
were going down a storm,
and they didn't have to charge tax
as the surface radiation kept them warm.
On the eighth day there were no planes in the sky,
we had street parties,
shared the last of our tins,
best china was brought out, bunting unfurled.
Armageddon?
'What's the problem?' we said,
'it's not the end of the world.'

Alternative Anthem

JOHN AGARD

Put the kettle on
Put the kettle on
It is the British answer
to Armageddon.

Never mind taxes rise
Never mind trains are late
One thing you can be sure of
and that's the kettle, mate.

It's not whether you lose
It's not whether you win
It's whether or not
you've plugged the kettle in.

May the kettle ever hiss
May the kettle ever steam
It is the engine
that drives our nation's dream.

Long live the kettle
that rules over us
May it be limescale free
and may it never rust.

Sing it on the beaches
Sing it from the housetops
The sun may set on empire
but the kettle never stops.

Everyone Hates the English

KIT WRIGHT

Everyone hates the English,
  Including the English. They sneer
At each other for being so English,
  So what are they doing here,
The English? It's *thick* with the English,
  All over the country. Why?
Anyone ever born English
  Should shut up, or fuck off, or die.

Anyone ever born English
  Should hold their extraction in scorn
And apologise all over England
  For ever at all being born,
For that's how it is, being English;
  Fodder for any old scoff
That England might be a nice country
  If only the English fucked off!

To a Mousse

W.N. HERBERT

O queen o sludge, maist royal mousse,
yir minions bear ye ben thi hoose,
O quakin sheikess, lavish, loose,
      dessert o fable:
ye pit thi bumps back oan ma goose
      and shauk ma table.

Ye lang cloacal loch o choc,
grecht flabby door at which Eh knock,
and wi ma spunie seek a lock
      tae mak ye gape,
ye flattened, tockless cuckoo clock
      that drives me ape.

Come let me lift ye tae ma mooth
and pree yir pertness wi ma tooth –
ye slake ma hunger and ma drouth
      wi wan sma bite:
come pang ma toomness tae thi outh
      wi broon delight.

Let ane and aa dig in thir spades
and cerve oot chocolate esplanades,
and raise thir umber serenades
      at ilka sip:
sweet Venus, queen o cocoa glades
      and thi muddied lip!

pang: stuff;
toomness: emptiness;
outh: utmost.

Address tae Chicken Tikka Masala

IRFAN MERCHANT

Fair fa' the nation's favourite dish
fulfilling everybody's wish,
great chieftain, O so very Scottish,
                    the spice o life;
ye came, and conquered the English,
                    tae cure the strife.

A myth of Glasgow's Shish Mahal
during Thatcher's iron rule,
your origins stretch to the Mughals
                    but when they tried
the chicken tikka the locals
                    found it too dry.

The chef wad think tae open up
a can o' Campbell's tomato soup,
add chilli, then colour with pap-
                    -rika for zest;
and then, O what a glorious sup,
                    simply the best.

As Scots we want the hottest thing
on the menu, a dish with zing:
haggis disnae mak us sing
                    we're globalised;
it's the mince an tatties o Tony Singh
                    brings tears tae eyes.

Noo we export tae India
oor national dish, making it clear
that Scotland is a warld leader
                          in aa the airts;
fir chicken tikka masala
                          ye've won oor hairts.

Lord Ganesha, tae please the Scots
remember whit they want is lots
o sauce and spices, very hot,
                          but dinnae worry;
Ah've got the answer in ma pot –
                          gie them a curry.

Tae a Selfie

*(Oan takin' a hunner fur
Facebook an' posting;
when pished)*

Oh my Goad, am feelin' great;
Aff tae the dance flair tae gyrate.
Oor kitchen's lookin' like a sea
Of glam an' glitter.
Am clingin' tae ma bevvy ticht
In case a slitter.

LORNA WALLACE

Sippin' oan ma rum an' juice;
A must admit, am feelin' loose,
And dinnae wahnt tae hink aboot
The morra's heid.
A pray an' hope ah'll be jist fine
Efter a feed.

Am lookin' smashin; whit a stunner!
A drain ma gless doon in a wunner
An' noo a really feel the need
Tae stert the show;
Grabbin' ma wee phone fur snaps;
We're gid tae go.

A summon aw ma lassies through
An' switch the camera tae front view;
An staun' an' gee ma ginger loacks
A soart and fix.
We huddle roon' an' wait tae hear
The fast wee clicks.

A shuffle roon' an' change ma stance;
We dae some shoats an' huv a dance,
A feel ma face is braw enough
Fur its ane shoot.
A stagger up and git a pal;
Am pished, nae doot.

Then in the moarn we congregate
An' wae deep breaths we face oor fate,
An' try tae fin' oot whit the Hell
We hink wint oan.
A drag ma erse oot of ma pit
An' check ma phone.

But then wan photie gee's me fright;
There must jist no huv bin gid light.
'Git that oaf; ah look like shite!'
Ah flap an' plead.
But a ken there's jist nae point;
It's oan 'News Feed'.

There's mare oanline, a look sae silly;
Am staunin' wae a blow-up wullie,
Ma cross-eyed heid is gazin'
Intae time an' space.
Aw shite, ah cannae quite believe
This fine disgrace.

A scrabble tae git them awa'
But hawf ma freens huv seen them aw,
An' noo a wish a hudnae been
Sae bloody steamin'.
Here come the comments fae ma maw;
Ma cheeks are beamin'.

Maw Broon Goes for Colonic Irrigation

JACKIE KAY

Maw Broon finds a new hobby
Says cheerio to the impacted jobby

Ye feel part o' ye falling awa – aw yer past,
yer mistakes, the daft lads ye winched afore Paw,
the wrang dresses, wrang recipes,
It a' fa's awa! Whit a lot there!
Hauf way thru the hale procedure
The man finds a bit of hough wha's endured
Tho ye hinny eaten potted hough fir – Och,
Years, years! Jings! Life takes odd turns.
Ye forget the times ye were black-affronted,
Said the wrang thing, had yer back agin the wa'.
(It's a wee straw, ye hardly feel it at a' – it's braw!)
Michty! It's a liberation, this colonic irrigation!
Aw o' a sudden yer auld body is a hale new nation,
Rid o' the parasites, clean as a whistle, yer saying *Ho-ho, gone*
                    yersell!
(And ye lose a hale stane.) The liquid they shoot up
Doesnae hauf stimulate evacuation! Better than a forty-day fast!
I'm telling ye! The past is the past is the past.
They used tae use a clyster syringe wey a rectal nozzle and plunger.
Crivens! Jings! I wis tempted tae dae it masell – (I'm ma ain
                    worst enemas)
baking soda, tap water, etc; but I thocht naw, Maw, treat yersell!
Yer a lang time deid: whit's the point saving fir a rainy day
When Auld Hough's rotting away in your bowels? *Away ye go!*
I'm awa tae buy a new hat in the sale. Whit a day! Whit a howl!

Omens

MARIN SORESCU

*translated from the Romanian
by* MICHAEL HAMBURGER

If you meet a chair,
that is good, you will go to Heaven.
If you meet a mountain,
that is bad, you'll go to the chair.
If you meet the Great Bear,
that is good, you will go to Heaven.
If you meet a snail,
that is bad, you'll go to the snail.
If you meet a woman,
that is good, you will go to Heaven.
If you meet a tablecloth,
that is bad, you will go to the cupboard.
If you meet a snake,
that is good, it will die and you'll go to Heaven.
If the snake meets you,
that is bad, you will die and the snake go to Heaven.

If you die,
that's bad, bad.

Beware of this omen
and of all others.

Lies My Mother Told Me

**ELIZABETH
THOMAS**

If you keep eating raw spaghetti
    you'll get pinworms,
    then I'll have to make
    a necklace of garlic for you to wear
    each night while you sleep,
    until they go away.
If you're mean to your younger brother, I'll know
    because I have a special eye
    that spies on you when I'm not home.
    You cannot hide from it,
    so don't try.
If you touch your 'down there'
    any time other than when using the toilet,
    your hand will turn green and fall off.
If you keep crossing your eyes
    they will stay that way
    until the wind
    changes direction.
It is bad luck to kill a moth. Moths are
    the souls of our ancestors and it just
    might be Papa paying a visit.
If you kiss a boy on the mouth
    your lips will stick together
    and he'll use the opportunity
    to suck out your brains.
If you ever lie to me
    God will know
    and rat you out.

And sometimes
God exaggerates.
Trust me –
you don't want that
to happen.

I Know This Because You Told Me

I'll break my neck if I jump again from the top of these stairs.
I'll suffer for the rest of my life in hospital
if I put my finger up my nose and then the wind changes.
I know this because you told me.

I'll drown if I jump once more in this nice muddy puddle,
there'll be a flash flood and the rain will rise and take us all.
The world should live in perfect harmony
and you'll kill the bloody neighbours if they don't trim their hedge.

CAROLINE BIRD

I should never swear, I know this because you told me.
If I talk to the teachers about our mortgage and the fact
that we don't pay our bills, then a monster will come out of the toilet
in the dead of night and pull me down.

You are not joking and only want to warn me. You are a good parent
and tell me life as it is, I know this because you told me.
If I fall in love at seventeen then it will not last.
If I eat too much I will explode and muck up your new shirt.

If I burp then I will blow myself inside out. The world
is quite a strange place and everyone is strange except you.
I know this because you told me.
If I take money from your wallet it is called crime,

if you take money from my piggy bank it is called borrowing.
If I never have a bath I will smell and people won't walk
on the same side of the street as me,
but if I do then I'll be sucked down the plug hole. Some women shave.

I know this because you told me. The banister is for holding,
not for sliding down and you were never rude to your parents.
I will break my neck if I jump again from the top of these stairs
and no, I should not do it anyway.

FROM

Going On

**PETER
READING**

This is unclean: to eat turbots on Tuesdays,
tying the turban unclockwise at cockcrow,
cutting the beard in a south-facing mirror,
wearing the mitre whilst sipping the Bovril,
chawing the pig and the hen and the ox-tail,
kissing of crosses with peckers erected,
pinching of bottoms (except in a yashmak),
flapping of cocks at the star-spangled-banner,
snatching the claret-pot off of the vicar,
munching the wafer without genuflexion,

facing the East with the arse pointing backwards,
thinking of something a little bit risqué,
raising the cassock to show off the Y-fronts,
holding a Homburg without proper licence,
chewing the cud with another man's cattle,
groping the ladies – or gentry – o'Sundays,
leaving the tip on the old-plum-tree-shaker,
speaking in physics instead of the Claptrap,
failing to pay due obeisance to monkeys,
loving the platypus more than the True Duck,
death without Afterlife, smirking in Mecca,
laughing at funny hats, holding the tenet
how that the Word be but fucking baloney,
failing to laud the Accipiter which Our Lord saith is Wisdom.

Started by *Australopithecus*, these are
time-honoured Creeds (and all unHoly doubters
shall be enlightened by Pious Devices:
mayhems of tinytots, low-flying hardwares,
kneecappings, letterbombs, deaths of the firstborns,
total extinctions of infidel unclean wrong-godded others).

For his Islamic enthusiasm, on the other hand, (William) Whiston was expelled from Cambridge in 1709

(From Orientalism *by Edward Said)*

JOHN GALLAS

My slipper'd tootsies roost along the grate.
The *damask* kettle sings. I conjugate
Moroccan verbs. My *iznik* coffeepot
Exhales the niff of Heav'n. The stairs do not.
Lokum twinkles on a *tunis* plate.
I puff my hubble-bubble. God is Great.

Outside, the fatuous, wat'ry *english* night
Cow'rs beneath the moon; the *Nazarite*
Dribbles in his tea; the captious wind
Persuades the *englishman* that he has sinn'd;
& wheezing organs, pinchèd guilt and sh—t
Deform the *Heart* into a *Hypocrite*.

I close the *baghdad* drapes. The clock chimes *Eight*.
I'm seventeen. It's dark. I contemplate
The Life to Come. My fretted *balkh*-lamps shine.
The rain drips down. I hear the sodden whine
of *chapel hymns*. I suck a *shiraz* date.
My tootsies glow and wiggle. God is Great.

How the Pope Is Chosen

JAMES TATE

Any poodle under ten inches high is a toy.
Almost always a toy is an imitation
of something grown-ups use.
Popes with unclipped hair are called *corded popes*.
If a Pope's hair is allowed to grow unchecked,
it becomes extremely long and twists
into long strands that look like ropes.
When it is shorter it is tightly curled.
Popes are very intelligent.
There are three different sizes.
The largest are called standard Popes.
The medium-sized ones are called miniature Popes.
I could go on like this, I could say:
'He is a squarely built Pope, neat,
well-proportioned, with an alert stance
and an expression of bright curiosity,'
but I won't. After a poodle dies
all the cardinals flock to the nearest 7-Eleven.
They drink Slurpies until one of them throws up
and then he's the new Pope.
He is then fully armed and rides through the wilderness alone,
day and night in all kinds of weather.
The new Pope chooses the name he will use as Pope,
like 'Wild Bill' or 'Buffalo Bill'.
He wears red shoes with a cross embroidered on the front.
Most Popes are called 'Babe' because
growing up to become a Pope is a lot of fun.
All the time their bodies are becoming bigger and stranger,
but sometimes things happen to make them unhappy.

They have to go to the bathroom by themselves,
and they spend almost all of their time sleeping.
Parents seem incapable of helping their little Popes grow up.
Fathers tell them over and over again not to lean out of windows,
but the sky is full of them.
It looks as if they are just taking it easy,
but they are learning something else.
What, we don't know, because we are not like them.
We can't even dress like them.
We are like red bugs or mites compared to them.
We think we are having a good time cutting cartoons out of the paper,
but really we are eating crumbs out of their hands.
We are tiny germs that cannot be seen under microscopes.
When a Pope is ready to come into the world,
we try to sing a song, but the words do not fit the music too well.
Some of the full-bodied Popes are a million times bigger than us.
They open their mouths at regular intervals.
They are continually grinding up pieces of the cross
and spitting them out. Black flies cling to their lips.
Once they are elected they are given a bowl of cream
and a puppy clip. Eyebrows are a protection
when the Pope must plunge through dense underbrush
in search of a sheep.

Superstition

MARIN SORESCU

translated from the
Romanian
by MICHAEL HAMBURGER

My cat washes
with her left paw,
there will be another war.

For I have observed
that whenever she washes
with her left paw
international tension grows
considerably.

How can she possibly keep her eye
on all the five continents?
Could it be
that in her pupils
that Pythia now resides
who has the power
to predict
the whole of history
without a full-stop or comma?

It's enough to make me howl
when I think that I
and the Heaven with its souls I have
shouldered
in the last resort
depend
on the whims of a cat.

Go and catch mice,
don't unleash
more world wars,
damned
lazybones!

Blandeur

KAY RYAN

If it please God,
let less happen.
Even out Earth's
rondure, flatten
Eiger, blanden
the Grand Canyon.
Make valleys
slightly higher,
widen fissures
to arable land,
remand your
terrible glaciers
and silence
their calving,
halving or doubling
all geographical features
toward the mean.
Unlean against our hearts.
Withdraw your grandeur
from these parts.

The Sounds of Earth

(broadcast from Voyager-II
to the universe)

JULIE O'CALLAGHAN

First, the most popular sound:
we call it talking – it is also known fondly as
shooting one's mouth off, discussing,
chewing the fat, yammering, blabbing,
conversing, confiding, debating, blabbing,
gossiping, hollering, and yakking.
So here's a whole bunch of jaw creakers.
How come none of you guys out there
don't yap at us – we'd sure like to hear
what you have to say
on the subject of where the hell you are.

For our second selection,
we will now play a medley of music
which you may or may not care for
since as I know myself
music is a very personal thing.
Why not aim a little musical extravaganza earthward?
As I say, we're waiting.

Now for our something-for-everyone finale.
Here's a rush hour traffic jam,
brakes are screeching – horns are blasting.
This is a phone ringing, a keyboard tapping,
and a printer whirring in the background.
I'm very partial to this next example of earth sounds:
a rocking chair creaking back and forth on a porch
accompanied by birds and crickets chirping.
To finish up, we've got a lawn mower,

knitting needles, a hammer, a saw,
a football stadium after a score,
a door shutting, a baby crying
and the ever-popular drone of television
blaring across the airways.

We're equal opportunity down here
so if you're a blob or have three heads
or look like something the cat dragged in –
we won't bat an eyelid.

Hotel Emergencies

BILL MANHIRE

The fire alarm sound: is given as a howling sound. Do not use
the lifts. The optimism sound: is given as the sound of a man
brushing his teeth. Do not go to bed. The respectability sound:
is given as a familiar honking sound. Do not run, do not sing.
The dearly-departed sound: is given as a rumble in the bones.
Do not enter the coffin. The afterlife sound: is given as the
music of the spheres. It will not reconstruct. The bordello
sound: is given as a small child screaming. Do not turn on the
light. The accident sound: is given as an ambulance sound.
You can hear it coming closer, do not crowd the footpaths.
The execution sound: is given as the sound of prayer. Oh be
cautious, do not stand too near

or you will surely hear: the machinegun sound, the weeping
mother sound, the agony sound, the dying child sound: whose
voice is already drowned by the approaching helicopter sound:

which is given as the dead flower sound, the warlord sound, the
hunting and fleeing and clattering sound, the amputation sound, the
bloodbath sound, the sound of the President quietly addressing his
dinner; now he places his knife and fork together (a polite and tidy
sound) before addressing the nation

and making a just and necessary war sound: which is given as a
freedom sound (do not cherish memory): which is given as a
security sound: which is given as a prisoner sound: which is given
again as a war sound: which is a torture sound and a watchtower
sound and a firing sound: which is given as a Timor sound: which
is given as a decapitation sound (do not think you will not gasp
tomorrow): which is given as a Darfur sound: which is given as a
Dachau sound: which is given as a dry river-bed sound, as a wind
in the poplars sound: which is given again as an angry god sound:

which is here as a Muslim sound: which is here as a Christian sound:
which is here as a Jewish sound: which is here as a merciful god
sound: which is here as a praying sound; which is here as a kneeling
sound: which is here as a scripture sound: which is here as a black-
wing sound: as a dark-cloud sound: as a black-ash sound: which is
given as a howling sound: which is given as a fire alarm sound:

which is given late at night, calling you from your bed (do not use the
lifts): which is given as a burning sound, no, as a human sound, as
a heartbeat sound: which is given as a sound beyond sound: which is
given as the sound of many weeping: which is given as an entirely
familiar sound, a sound like no other, up there high in the smoke
above the stars

Static City

DEAN YOUNG

Some of us sitting around listening to static
and one says, That's nothing compared to the sixties' static.
What are you talking about? says another.
If you want real static you got to go way back,
to Memphis, like when Memphis was still
Egyptian, people still with both eyes
on one side of their nose like flounders
wandering around like wind-up toys
before anyone even knew what static was,
before even the wah-wah pedal as we know it,
bread like 2 cents a loaf, before shag carpet
and modern recording techniques
where you don't like something just flick a number.
What we had back then was crawdad boil.
And rope.
And a couple guys at the crossroads
who sold their souls to a snake,
a fucking snake, man,
because they didn't have nothing else
a snake could use and even if they did.
Absolutely no electric tuning forks,
no designer cowboy shirts,
no atom bombs small enough
to fit in a fucking suitcase, man,
but they had an inkling,
a cerebral spark from knocking their heads
against a wall so long they were getting the idea
that the wall was just an idea, a concept
you could just pass right through

but then there'd be another wall
like when you get through childhood
and there's puberty,
it's walls all the way, man,
but they had this authentic buzz,
a hive in the hedgerows
and when a talking snake offers,
you deal, man, you don't
zigzag prevaricate
because that's the snake's metier,
you just deal even if no one'll ever know your name
except a few devotees,
oddball ex-cons, misfits with no gas money,
maybe only a couple on the planet at any one time
knowing the true static
behind this stepped-on, pooched-out
beep beep thunk thunk fluff
everyone's plugged into now,
propagating like cellophane,
like it's raining diamonds on the wedding parade,
like it's god's first thought
and they were around to hear it
and it didn't grate their brains like cheese
which it would, man,
you'd hit the dirt,
everything ripping up your heart
like a horse that wants to head home
only home's on fire and your mind's the fire
so all you can do is rub dirt into the fire

which is your mind like I said.
And you're telling me you ask
someone like that for identification?
No, man, you just know
or you don't and if you don't
you won't ever. Imagine a frog
in your mouth, struggling.
Now imagine you're that frog.

The All Purpose Country and Western Self Pity Song

KIT WRIGHT

He jumped off the box-car
In Eastbourne, the beast born
In him was too hungry to hide:

His neck in grief's grommet,
He groaned through his vomit
At the churn
And the yearn
At the turn
Of the tide.

He headed him soon
For a sad-lit saloon
In back of the edge of the strand,
Where a man almost ended
Sat down and extended

His speckled,
Blue-knuckled
And cuckolded
Hand.

Cried, The wind broke my marriage in two.
Clean through the bones of it,
Christ how it blew!
I got no tomorrow
And sorrow
Is tough to rescind:
So forgive me if I should break wind, son,
Forgive me
If I should break wind.

At this the bartender
Addressed the agenda,
A dish-cloth kept dabbing his eye.
Said, Pardon intrusion
Upon your effusion
Of loss but none wooed it
Or rued it
As I.

For after the eve of Yvonne,
My God, how it hurts now the woman has gone!
Heart-sick as a dog,
I roll on like a log

Down the roaring black river
Where once sailed
A swan.

Then the dog on the floor,
Who'd not spoken before,
Growled, Ain't it the truth you guys said?
I may be a son–
Of-a-bitch but that bitch

Was my Sun
And she dumped me,
The bitch did,
For dead.

So three lonely guys in the night and a hound
Drank up, and they headed them out to the Sound,
Threw up, then they threw themselves
In and they
Drowned.

      O dee-o-dayee...
      O dee-o-dayee...
      Woe-woe-dalayee...

thwok

(a game in the life)

MATT HARVEY

bounce bounce bounce bounce
thwackety wackety zingety ping
hittety backety pingety zang
wack, thwok, thwack, pok
thwikety, thwekity, thwokity, thwakity
cover the court with alarming alacrity
smackety dink, smackety dink
boshety bashity crotchety crashety
up loops a lob with a teasing temerity
leaps in the air in defiance of gravity
puts it away with a savage severity
coupled with suavity
nice
15–love
(reaches for towel with a certain serenity)

bounce, bounce, bounce, bounce
thwack, thwok, plak, plok
come to the nettety
bit of a liberty
quickly regrettety
up goes a lobbity
hoppety skippety
awkwardly backwardly
slippety trippety
tumble & sprawl
audible gasps…
15–all

(opponent asks how is he?
courtesy, nice to see
getting up gingerly
brushity thighsity
all, if you're asking me
bit big-girls-blousity)

bounce bounce bounce
whack, thwok, plik, plok
into the corner, then down the linety
chasety downity, whackety backety
all on the runnity, crossety courtety
dropety vollety – quality, quality...
... oh I say what impossible gettery
no, umpirical rulery   nottety uppity –
oooh – doesn't look happety
back to the baseline
muttery muttery muttery muttery
30–15

bounce, bounce, bounce,
thwacketty OUT
bounce, bounce, bounce,
thwacketty BLEEP
2nd serve
bounce, bounce, bounce,
thwacketty – slappity

thwackety thumpity
dinkety-clinkety, gruntity-thumpity
clinkety
thump!
30-all
fistety pumpety, fistety pumpety COME ON!

quiet please
bounce, bounce, bounce,
thwacketty thwoketty
bashetty boshetty
clashety closhety
OUT!
what?
lookaty linety, lookaty line-judge
line judge nodity
wearily query
umpire upholdery, indicate inchery
insult to injury
give line judge scrutiny
face full of mutiny,
40–30
back to the baseline
through gritted teethery
muttery mutiny mutiny muttery

bounce bounce bounce
thwak, thwok, thwak, plok
thwakety plik, thwoketty plak
to-ity fro-ity fro-ity to-ity
slowity quickety quickety slowity
turnety headety, headety turnity
leftety rightety leftety rightety
seems like we've been here a bloomin eternity
rightety leftety rightety leftety
topety spinnety, backhandy slicety
lookety watchety, scratchety bottity
fabulous forehand, backhandy slicety
furious forehand, savagely slicety
fearsome ferocity, vicious velocity
bilious backhand – blasted so blistery…
…half a mile out but that line judge is history
OOOWWWWWWWWT!

GAME
new balls please

The Black Wet

W.N. HERBERT

It's raining stair-rods and chairlegs,
it's raining candelabra and microwaves,
it's raining eyesockets.
When the sun shines through the shower
it's raining the hair of Sif,
each strand of which is real gold
(carat unknown).

It's raining jellyfish,
it's raining nuts, bolts and pineal glands,
it's raining a legion of fly noyades,
it's raining marsupials and echnidae,
it's raining anoraks in profusion.
It's siling, it's spittering, it's stotting, it's teeming,
it's pouring, it's snoring, it's plaining, it's Spaining.

People look up, open their mouths momentarily,
and drown.
People look out of windows and say,
'Send it down, David.'
Australians remark, 'Huey's missing the bowl.'
Americans reply, 'Huey, Dewie and Louie
are missing the bowl.'

It is not merely raining,
it's Windering and Thirling, it's Buttering down.
It's raining lakes, it's raining grass-snakes,
it's raining Bala, Baikal, and balalaikas,
it's raining soggy sidewinders and sadder adders.

It's raining flu bugs, Toby jugs and hearth-rugs,
it's raining vanity.

The sky is one vast water-clock
and it's raining seconds, it's raining years:
already you have spent more of your life looking at the rain
that you have sleeping, cooking, shopping and making love.
It's raining fusilli and capeletti,
it's raining mariners and albatrosses,
it's raining iambic pentameters.

Let's take a rain-check:
it's raining houndstooth and pinstripe,
it's raining tweed. This is the tartan of McRain.
This is the best test of the wettest west:
it is not raining locusts – just.
Why rain pests
when you can rain driving tests?

It is raining through the holes in God's string vest.

NOTE: *The black wet*
(Scots) – rain as
opposed to snow.

The Man in the Comic Strip

LIZ LOCHHEAD

For the man in the comic strip
things are not funny. No wonder he's
running in whichever direction his pisspoor
piston legs are facing
getting nowhere fast.

If only he had the sense he was born with
he'd know there is a world of difference
between the thinks bubble and the speech balloon
and when to keep it zipped, so, with a visible fastener –
But his mouth is always getting him into trouble.
Fistfights blossom round him,
there are flowers explode when the punches connect.
A good idea is a light bulb, but too seldom.
When he curses, spirals
and asterisks and exclamation marks
whizz around his head like his always palpable distress.
Fear comes off him like petals from a daisy.
Anger brings lightning down on his head and
has him hopping.
Hunger fills the space around him
with floating ideograms of roasted chickens
and iced buns like maidens' breasts the way
the scent of money fills his eyes with dollar signs.

For him the heart is always a beating heart,
True Love –
always comically unrequited.
The unmistakable silhouette of his one-and-only
will always be kissing another
behind the shades at her window
and, down-at-the-mouth, he'll
always have to watch it from the graphic
lamplit street.

He never knows what is around the corner,
although we can see it coming.
When he is shocked his hair stands perfectly on end
but his scream is a total zero and he knows it.
Knows to beware of the zigzags of danger,
knows how very different from
the beeline of zees that is a hostile horizontal buzzing
of singleminded insects swarming after him
are the gorgeous big haphazard zeds of sleep.

Convinced by a Nalungiaq Song

DEAN YOUNG

Back in the earliest days,
a person could become an animal
and an animal a person
so sometimes the animals were people
and the people animals
and it made no difference.
Sometimes the person drank the wine,
sometimes the wine the person
and you'd wake up in a heap of puffins,
not feeling this dreadful falling off
and piling up that we've come to call
normal life, pronouncements
stacked by the doorstops
to be assessed and kicked through,
the gym full of nymphs showing off their implants,
fat spiders and shorter days,
apparatchicks issuing demerits.
In the earliest days
there was no nagging question
of What do I do? and never
enough time to do it,
Where do I belong? and How
can I get away? Rain
was a horizontal lake
you'd float in, fog
in fog slippers sneaking off the path,

shaking the smallest of bells.
And when night came as a black bird,
you were another black bird
and no one tried to strap a message to your leg
or make you repeat a stupid phrase
or honk while you tried to parallel park
or tell you how to cook your own heart
while lecturing you on etiquette.
When night came in its night-spattered cloak,
you'd put on your star pajamas
and vanish into it
and it would vanish into you.

Goat

JO SHAPCOTT

Dusk, deserted road, and suddenly
I was a goat. To be truthful, it took
two minutes, though it seemed sudden,
for the horns to pop out of my skull,
for the spine to revolutionise and go
horizontal, for the fingers to glue
together and for the nails to become
important enough to upgrade to hoof.
The road was not deserted any more, but full
of goats, and I liked that, even though I hate
the rush hour on the tube, the press of bodies.
Now I loved snuffling behind his or her ear,
licking a flank or two, licking and snuffling here,

there, wherever I liked. I lived for the push
of goat muscle and goat bone, the smell of goat fur,
goat breath and goat sex. I ended up on the edge
of the crowd where the road met the high
hedgerow with the scent of earth, a thousand
kinds of grass, leaves and twigs, flower-heads
and the intoxicating tang of the odd ring-pull
or rubber to spice the mixture. I wanted
to eat everything. I could have eaten the world
and closed my eyes to nibble at the high
sweet leaves against the sunset. I tasted
that old sun and the few dark clouds
and some tall buildings far away in the next town.
I think I must have swallowed an office block
because this grinding enormous digestion tells me
it's stuck on an empty corridor which has
at the far end, I know, a tiny human figure.

It Happens Like This

JAMES TATE

I was outside St Cecilia's Rectory
smoking a cigarette when a goat appeared beside me.
It was mostly black and white, with a little reddish
brown here and there. When I started to walk away,
it followed. I was amused and delighted, but wondered
what the laws were on this kind of thing. There's
a leash law for dogs, but what about goats? People
smiled at me and admired the goat. 'It's not my goat,'

I explained. 'It's the town's goat. I'm just taking
my turn caring for it.' 'I didn't know we had a goat,'
one of them said. 'I wonder when my turn is.' 'Soon,'
I said. 'Be patient. Your time is coming.' The goat
stayed by my side. It stopped when I stopped. It looked
up at me and I stared into its eyes. I felt he knew
everything essential about me. We walked on. A police-
man on his beat looked us over. 'That's a mighty
fine goat you got there,' he said, stopping to admire.
'It's the town's goat,' I said. 'His family goes back
three-hundred years with us,' I said, 'from the beginning.'
The officer leaned forward to touch him, then stopped
and looked up at me. 'Mind if I pat him?' he asked.
'Touching this goat will change your life,' I said.
'It's your decision.' He thought real hard for a minute,
and then stood up and said, 'What's his name?' 'He's
called the Prince of Peace,' I said. 'God! This town
is like a fairy tale. Everywhere you turn there's mystery
and wonder. And I'm just a child playing cops and robbers
forever. Please forgive me if I cry.' 'We forgive you,
Officer,' I said. 'And we understand why you, more than
anybody, should never touch the Prince.' The goat and
I walked on. It was getting dark and we were beginning
to wonder where we would spend the night.

From
My Rough
Goatbook

JOHN WHITWORTH

Every goat has his day but when crime doesn't pay
Even half a goat's better than none.
Fine words butter no parsnips nor turnips nor gymslips.
You can't get a goat with a gun.

As you sow, so you reap, if still waters run deep,
It'll turn out all right on the goatnight.
So no news is good news and you've nothing to lose
When his butt's so much worse than his goatbite.

Yes, hard liquor is quicker but don't tell the vicar,
He only came here for the beer.
What's as good as a nudge is he's drunk as a judge,
It's as plain as the goat in your car.

But a rolling goat gathers no birds of a feather,
The early goat catches the carrot,
If you win the cigar it's worth two in the car,
You can't make a silk goat from a parrot.

Pluck your goat in the bud, you old stick-in-the-mud,
See your chances go up like a rocket,
Time and goats wait for no man, you roam in the gloaming
And end with a hole in your pocket

And a goat in your soul (meaning two in the hole)
That you need like a butt in the head,
So it's out of the samovar into the abattoir,
Never say goat till you're dead.

Still, a word to the wise, they don't come in your size
And I'd rather be billy than clever.
When a goat mows a meadow he casts a long shadow.
For ever and ever and ever.

DSS Dream

MARTÍN ESPADA

I dreamed
the Department of Social Services
came to the door and said:
'We understand
you have a baby,
a goat and a pig living here
in a two-room apartment.
This is illegal.
We have to take the baby away,
unless you eat the goat.'

'The pig's OK?' I asked.
'The pig's OK,' they said.

The Joy Attendant on the Little Journey

RUSSELL EDSON

A man was gradually turning into a swine. And at the same time trying to put his affairs in order.

As he lay in his own turds he was trying to think. But it was getting harder and harder...

Now let me see, he would think, should I hire a swineherd, or a chauffeur? Of course I shall eventually end up at the slaughterhouse. Looking forward to it. Perhaps I should hire a hearse? I must make arrangements while I can still think. For instance, will such a little journey demand a funeral? – A journey completed when I have come apart in hams and various cuts of loin, picnic shoulders, spareribs, bacon; perhaps even sausage.

– Lard? Oh yes, I should hope lots of that. And fatback, too...

Counting Sheep

RUSSELL EDSON

A scientist has a test tube full of sheep. He wonders if he should try to shrink a pasture for them.

They are like grains of rice.

He wonders if it is possible to shrink something out of existence.

He wonders if the sheep are aware of their tininess, if they have any sense of scale. Perhaps they just think the test tube is a glass barn...

He wonders what he should do with them; they certainly have less meat and wool than ordinary sheep. Has he reduced their commercial value?

He wonders if they could be used as a substitute for rice, a sort of woolly rice...

He wonders if he just shouldn't rub them into a red paste between his fingers.

He wonders if they're breeding, or if any of them have died.

He puts them under a microscope and falls asleep counting them.

Sheep

(for @dogsdoingthings)

**CHRISSY
WILLIAMS**

Sheep wearing short pink diner uniforms, serving coffee, startling easily.

Sheep being followed through evening streets, sensing danger, flocking helplessly.

Sheep afraid in the nightclub chaos, hooves on the table, staring blankly.

Sheep in the jaws of persistent death, hearing *come with me if you want to live.*

Sheep on the run being told of the lamb that's yet to be born, the essential future.

Sheep hysterical, laughing, incredulous. Domestic sheep who
can't balance a chequebook.

Sheep being taught to make household bombs, to fire guns,
weave steel wool.

Sheep growing up on a motel bed. Sheep counting sheep, making
love before dawn.

Sheep being blown from a tank's explosion, fighting metal with
flesh, nearing exhaustion.

Sheep left nosing their lover's limp body. Sheep pulling them-
selves up. Sheep finishing it.

Sheep driving with a shotgun on the empty seat, their own dogs
for protection, as the new life kicks.

Lies

JO SHAPCOTT

In reality, sheep are brave, enlightened
and sassy. They are walking clouds
and like clouds have forgotten
how to jump. As lambs they knew.
Lambs jump because in their innocence
they still find grass exciting.
Some turf is better for tiptoeing

say the lambs. Springy meadows
have curves which invite fits
of bouncing and heel-kicking
to turn flocks of lambs
into demented white spuds boiling in the pot.
Then there is a French style of being a lamb
which involves show and a special touch
at angling the bucking legs. Watch carefully
next time: Lambs love to demonstrate –
you won't have to inveigle.
Eventually, of course, lambs grow trousers
and a blast of wool
which keeps them anchored to the sward.
Then grass is first and foremost
savoury, not palpable.
I prefer the grown sheep: even when damp
she is brave, enlightened and sassy,
her eye a kaleidoscope of hail and farewell,
her tail her most eloquent organ of gesture.
When she speaks, it is to tell me
that she is under a spell, polluted.
Her footwear has been stolen
and the earth rots her feet.
In reality she walks across the sky
upside down in special pumps.

Love Song with a Flock of Sheep

JO SHAPCOTT

'Win a flock of sheep' said the advertisement.
'Sheep Dip: an eight year old pure malt whisky.
You will find an entry form on every bottle.'

I will. I will buy the whisky,
I will find the entry form. I will:
I will win the sheep and I'll give them to you.

Keep the flock at home
and let them graze around the house.
Kindly and damp, they'll eat the carpet
and will start on the wallpaper too;
your interior decorations will be masticated away.
The flock is softer than soft furnishings
but when they've eaten all that they'll start
on the hard stuff. They'll munch their way
through the mantelpiece and everything –
your books, your manuscripts –
will fly into their placid mouths.

I know you. You'll like it better without
all that ruminated stuff. You want
the woolly life, carding and spinning,
with only sheep for furniture and bedclothes.
The flock will find you out eventually
and start their blowing in your ears
and their nuzzling across your hair.
It will begin in the kitchen with a fleecy
brush along the backs of your knees.

They'll surround you on the sofa
and drink out of your bath. Your clothes
will go into the three stomachs and in the dark
you'll feel sheep nibble between your toes
and suck your toenails. They will graze
your legs, removing every hair with teeth
so precise and shy you'll feel only
a mist of breath and lips. They'll move
in a cloud across your chest, your belly,
face and beard – everywhere – cropped
down to a downy stubble, peaceful as pasture.
Soon you will be as shorn as a yearling lamb
and twice as happy, blissoming with the flock.

When I arrive, dressed as Bo-Peep,
I won't get a look in. But by hook or by crook
you shall have them anyway: sheep fleecy, sheep shorn
and me lovelorn.

Sheep Piece

DERYN REES-JONES

I *The couple*

Remember the photo the sheep took of us?
My face made tentative and ugly in the sun,

and you in the shirt that would've matched your eyes,
except that you were (humbly?)

looking at the ground?
We couldn't understand a word she said,

but somehow, as it came about, there was no need
for spoken promises or speeches, no need

for *Smile, please!* or a grudging
teeth-clenched *Cheese!* In a sheepish way

we looked and locked so perfectly together –
my flowing bright blue skirt hitched up,

my shoelaces, my plaited hair, undone.
And I really can't remember why we got down on our knees

except we weren't quite able to believe
– who could – in such a sudden, perfect

kind of love, or even in ourselves,
that summer, let alone the sheep,

the coloured Polaroid emerging
and all the attendant angels fussing round.

II *The sheep*

As if four legs were an eternal condemnation
to a horizontal life! As if they'd never seen
a sheep before, gone vertical! They thought

I was a god, the tightened curls of my golden coat
shining and radiant. Not a rare breed,
badger-faced or speckled, just a local,
newly-washed and happy, afro-combed.
And yet it was as if I was about
to steal their souls, the way they looked at me,
so innocent, like children
as they prayed there on the stubbly
sheep-chewed ground. And then, another thing,
they were amazed I shared a language with them,
rated their technologies, could wield a Kodak
good as any other sheep. They blinked and
shuffled, finding I was eloquent, a little bossy,
charming, perspicacious, sometimes rude. But
proud of sheep-heritage, glad to be ruminant
and beardless, progressive, self-controlled...

(Okay, I was an amateur, but it was just
that moment that I wanted:
them making sheep's eyes
as the sun, glowing behind them,
slipped gently through the trees.)

III *The photograph*

Funny how it starts. With an itch
when it's least expected. How it spreads
like a blush would, on a body of velvet,

a spreading soft discordance
edging slowly through the spectrum
until you are a shiny hard oasis
sucking all the colours in.
You have to make yourself remember
how you always start from scratch
before your features decompose
into dimensions, all
your plain, white surface areas confused.
You have to tell yourself
it's only transient, until
like chameleon, you find
you're doing it again, with someone,
something else. Being a woman, now,
and smaller than she'd thought,
and younger, a man, quite boyish
and wild-haired. That's when you start to hurt,
feeling the strain of everything contained,
each particle, each colour. You're not
yourself, the photographic paper or
the thing you photographed:
the lovers or the landscape.
Not the moment when you stole them either,
all that bemusement and contentment,
all those colours, all that joy,
ventriloquised imperfectly, so perfectly:
flesh-coloured flesh. The girl, the boy.

Spiritual Chickens

STEPHEN DOBYNS

A man eats a chicken every day for lunch,
and each day the ghost of another chicken
joins the crowd in the dining room. If he could
only see them! Hundreds and hundreds of spiritual
chickens, sitting on chairs, tables, covering
the floor, jammed shoulder to shoulder. At last
there is no more space and one of the chickens
is popped back across the spiritual plain to the earthly.
The man is in the process of picking his teeth.
Suddenly there's a chicken at the end of the table,
strutting back and forth, not looking at the man
but knowing he is there, as is the way with chickens.
The man makes a grab for the chicken but his hand
passes right through her. He tries to hit the chicken
with a chair and the chair passes through her.
He calls in his wife but she can see nothing.
This is his own private chicken, even if he
fails to recognise her. How is he to know
this is a chicken he ate seven years ago
on a hot and steamy Wednesday in July,
with a little tarragon, a little sour cream?
The man grows afraid. He runs out of his house
flapping his arms and making peculiar hops
until the authorities take him away for a cure.
Faced with the choice between something odd
in the world or something broken in his head,
he opts for the broken head. Certainly,
this is safer than putting his opinions
in jeopardy. Much better to think he had

imagined it, that he had made it happen.
Meanwhile, the chicken struts back and forth
at the end of the table. Here she was, jammed in
with the ghosts of six thousand dead hens, when
suddenly she has the whole place to herself.
Even the nervous man has disappeared. If she
had a brain, she would think she had caused it.
She would grow vain, egotistical, she would
look for someone to fight, but being a chicken
she can just enjoy it and make little squawks,
silent to all except the man who ate her,
who is far off banging his head against a wall
like someone trying to repair a leaky vessel,
making certain that nothing unpleasant gets in
or nothing of value falls out. How happy
he would have been to be born a chicken,
to be of good use to his fellow creatures
and rich in companionship after death.
As it is he is constantly being squeezed
between the world and his idea of the world.
Better to have a broken head — why surrender
his corner on truth? — better just to go crazy.

The Man Whose Left Hand Thought It Was a Chicken

TIFFANY ATKINSON

did some things remarkably well, like
catching flies and finding dropped earrings
or contact lenses. Others – making omelettes
say – he learned to perform with his left hand
deep in a pocketful of seed. Mere incidentals
if your arm does chicken from the elbow down.
At times, for sure, sheer cock: up well before
he was, especially if his woman was in town,
cock-hand was known to arc at strangers in the pub
or jump soft objects. Shopping for fruit with cock-
hand was no joke. But there was hen-hand too,
heat-seeking, full of mild compulsions. This bird
knew a thing or two about the secret berries of
his lover's flesh, the dust-bowl of her back. And
rumbled the acorn growing in her breast, and fluttered
at her cheekbones till she slept. Then for the kids
alone, the crazy bantam-hand of knock-knocks,
now-you-see-its. Still. To say the sun's play through
his fingers made the brightest comb, to say he
crossed the road more often than required, to say
he only ever drove an automatic, never got promoted
and was photographed more often than he liked, to
say he almost had his own eye out a hundred times
is not to say the man was not his own man. No. He
was a flock of tangents and surprises. And without
him we have lost all memory, all possibility of flight.

The Chicken Variations

KEN SMITH

Chicken calling:

Whisky Oscar Chicken. Whisky Oscar Chicken
calling Foxtrot, come in Foxtrot.

This is Whisky Oscar Chicken
calling Foxtrot, come in Foxtrot.

Chicken faith:

The word was let there be chicken.
Before the chicken was the chicken,
before the egg was the egg,
from the beginning of the word the word was chicken.

And before that the word was egg.
And before that the word was still egg.
And before that the great sky chicken
who is the rooster and hen mother of us all.

Phrases for translation:

Excuse me, parlez-vous chicken ici?
Please, where is the cambio for live chickens?
Is this the fast chicken for Bratislava?
Bitte, do you have a place I can leave my broody hen?
I am married with a roost and three chicks,

I live in Little Red Rooster Town, Minnesota.
I was born in the Year of the Chicken
under the sign of the Chicken, have a nice day.
I would like chicken en suite, por favor.
Chicken on the rocks, chicken all round.
It's my turn for the Lakenvelder meine Damen und Herren.
S'il vous plaît m'sieur I want the Chicken Cab Co.
I would like a bottle of this Chateau Poulet Blanc.
This chicken is too loud, take it away please.
Entschuldige, I have to go buy a chicken now.
Pardon me, I think my chicken is on fire.
I have a one way ticket to Chickenville, goodbye.

Let us consider the chicken:

Lately I've been thinking about the chickens,
clucking their peevish lives out in the long batteries,
where the lights shorten the days, nothing changes,
it's hell on earth and every one in here is loo-loo.

Even in a yard they fret, always at the edge,
suspicious, laying the great egg, staring, watching,
wary for the cockbird or pecking at their dinners
or asleep dreaming worms, slugs, fat maggots.

And then they die, all of them without names,
numbers, without biographies, votes, pension rights,
their throats routinely cut, stripped, chopped up,
cooked in a pot with onions and peppers and devoured.

Chuck. Chuck. The Hungarians, who got them
from the Bulgarians, they say *tyuk. Tyuk tyuk tyuk.*
Comrades, clearly this is not in the chickens' interest.
Our feathered friends are manifestly at a disadvantage.

And no one protests, no one gives a Gypsy's gob
for all their aspirations, dreams, their brief itchy lives
scratching and complaining, part of the food chain.

Save the chicken. Save the chicken.

Chicken lore:

For a start there was the Miracle of the Cocks and Hens,
there was the Parable of the White Leghorn,
there was the Cockadoodledoo Revelation at Alexandria,
there was the Exemplary Lesson of the Rhode Island Reds,
there was the Sermon on the Flightless Gallinacae,
there was the Bantam Capon Culture of the Po Valley,
there was the Black Langshan Khanate of Kiev,
there was the Coxcomb Dynasty of the Mekong Delta,
there was the Teaching of Salvatore Stefano Cacciatore,
there was the Red Rooster Crusade of 1332,
there was the Most Noble Order of Jersey Black Giants,
there was the Barred Plymouth Rock Declaration,
there was the Constitution of the Andalusian Blues,
there was the Divine Sisterhood of Old Poultry Lane,
there was the secret conclave of the Orpington Buffs,

there was La Flèche, Crèvecœur, Campine, Faverolle,
there was the whole mighty host of Gallus Domesticus
migrating out of the east, crossing the windy steppes
clutched in the armpits of savage horsemen,
and there was blood, there were mountains of skulls.
We were at Marathon, at Agincourt, on the Somme,
we were the Wild Chickens who fought at Malplaquet.
We too had our epics, our ten year return to Ithaca
only to find strangers clucking in our compound.
We too had our blind poets Homer and Milton.
There was Chaucer's *The Dream of Fair Chickens*,
there was the Last Lay of the Fighting Cocks,
there was the Black Virgin of the Chickenshack,
there was Shakespeare's famous Chicken Soliloquy,
there was the patriarch Chicken Joe Bailey,
there was the saint and martyr Adolphus Chicken,
there was the inventor and explorer Gustavus Chicken,
there was the hero Lieutenant General Gordon Chicken,
there was Captain Bingo 'Chickenwings' Benson
who saved us again and again from foreign invasion,
there was the gunfighter Roaring Jack Chicken,
there was the horn player Willy Bantam Chicken,
there was the Ode to a Chicken and the Air on a Chicken,
there was the Chicken Sonata, the Chicken Symphony,
there was Chicken Blues, there was Chicken Boogie,
there was the Chicken Domesday, the Cockcrow Manifesto
the Chicken Coop Oath, the Last Address to the Chickens,
there was the chicken round dance and chicken chants,
there were chicken fiestas and chicken olympics,

there was Chicken Rococo and Chicken Gothic,
there was the Colegio Pollo of medieval Florence,
there were the *Chicken Études* of Guillaume Apollinaire,
there was the School of Contemporary Chicken Studies,
there was the Distressed Indigent Chickens' Benevolent Society,
there were the Thoughts of The Cocksman Chairman Charlie,
there was the Theory and Evolution of the Chicken,
there was the architecture of Frank Lloyd Chicken,
there was Henry Ford's Chicken Mass Production System,
and it says here much else besides, all of it now best forgot.

Saith the Sky Chicken:

Woe to those who sell guns
amongst the warring states.
Woe to those who shell the wounded.

Woe to those who take another's house,
and say *this is my farm, these my chickens,*
who pick up the photo album and say
why these are all my relatives.

Interim conclusions:

What is a mere chicken to do?
Everything you see belongs to the Fat Man.
The true commonwealth of equals is now very far off.
The Dark Ages begin again any time now.

I'll tell you this: the Hundred Years' War
did nothing for those who eat worms.
What use was the Renaissance?
The Revolution's been and gone.

Last bulletin:

The barbarians are at the city's throat,
their tanks moving down the great ringroads,
the anti-chicken forces are all around us.
Any second now there will be no more electricity.

This is the end of the Chicken Road.
This is the last hour of the Chicken Republic.
This is the final demise of the Chicken Revolution.
This is the end of all chicken civilisation.

And this is Radio Free Chicken signing off.
Goodbye Foxtrot, Goodbye Tango Charlie.
We of the Chicken Coalition salute you.
We of the Chicken Millennium bid you adieu.

Cow

SELIMA HILL

I want to be a cow
and not my mother's daughter.
I want to be a cow
and not in love with you.
I want to feel free to feel calm.
I want to be a cow who never knows
the kind of love you 'fall in love with' with;
a queenly cow, with hips as big and sound
as a department store,
a cow the farmer milks on bended knee,
who when she dies will feel dawn
bending over her like lawn to wet her lips.

I want to be a cow,
nothing fancy –
a cargo of grass,
a hammock of soupy milk
whose floating and rocking and dribbling's undisturbed
by the echo of hooves to the city;
of crunching boots;
of suspicious-looking trailers parked on verges;
of unscrupulous restaurant-owners
who stumble, pink-eyed, from stale beds
into a world of lobsters and warm telephones;
of streamlined Japanese freighters
ironing the night,
heavy with sweet desire like bowls of jam.

The Tibetans have 85 words for states of consciousness.
This dozy cow I want to be has none.
She doesn't speak.
She doesn't do housework or worry about her appearance.
She doesn't roam.
Safe in her fleet
of shorn-white-bowl-like friends,
she needs, and loves, and's loved by,
only this –
the farm I want to be a cow on too.

Don't come looking for me.
Don't come walking out into the bright sunlight
looking for me,
black in your gloves and stockings and sleeves
and large hat.
Don't call the tractorman.
Don't call the neighbours.
Don't make a special fruit-cake for when I come home:
I'm not coming home.
I'm going to be a cowman's counted cow.
I'm going to be a cow
and you won't know me.

The Metempsychosis of the Yak

GUS FERGUSON

He has no house, he has no shack,
Just shaggy hair upon his back
That hangs from cranium to hoof –
An absolutely perfect roof
To shelter him from winter chills
Amongst the Himalayan hills.

Tibetans ride upon the backs
Of generous and gentle yaks
Who offer milk; their hair for rope,
Their flesh for meat, their fat for soap,
And listen as the valley swells
In irony to temple bells

That toll that karmic law decrees
They will return as Red Chinese.

A Prodigy of Nature

FRANK KUPPNER

As the mighty herd of bison stampeded across the plain,
on one of those (to the outsider) unintelligible
impulses which seem to inspire them, resembling
a mindless panic as much as anything else;
one of the beasts near the back turned to his neighbour –
on the left – or was it the right? – and said to him:
'You know, my friend: this process begins to worry me.
I think I recognise broadly where we are.

The fact is, if I'm right, then very soon
we reach a cliff hereabouts; and, should we get there
at this speed, then we'll all be over the top
and dead, before we can even begin to slow down.
It's playing on my nerves, I don't mind telling you.'
To which the second, frowning, with sage demeanour replied:
'Look, mate. What do you or I know about these things?
We're not the leaders, are we? No. Strike a light!
Okay? Screw the bobbin! We are nowhere near the front.
It's for others to make those decisions, and for us
to follow them as responsibly as we can.
You this way, we this way too, if you take my drift.
Not abdicating our critical faculties –
no; I'm not saying that; certainly we must
retain our nerve and judgement – however, *au fond*,
we can't do it all ourselves, can we? No; we can't.
We have to trust the powers-that-be in a case like this.
We cannot decipher the whole world for ourselves.
Why would they call this a plain if it isn't flat?
It's sheer common sense. I'm not unsympathetic –
no, friend; I am by no means lacking sympathy
with your point of view – but events are moving so fast
we must go with them.' 'Right. Fair enough,' said his colleague,
as they disappeared in their turn head-first over the precipice.

Horse Music

MATTHEW SWEENEY

Hearing of horses speaking Irish on the island
he took a boat out there, paid an islander
daft money to lead him to the westernmost field
where a shy pair of russet ponies stood head-
to head on a hilly mound that jutted out over
the leaping froth of the Atlantic. He pretended
not to notice them, said goodbye to his guide
in Irish picked up from books in southern Spain –
his lifetime's hobby – then sat on his hunkers,
listening hard, but either the horses were quiet
or he needed to get closer. He waited until a
gang of screaking gulls got the horses neighing,
then over he went, soothing them with murmurs,
stroking them, until one said in fluent Irish
to the other 'This hairy fellow could be OK,
but we can't trust him, can't trust any of them.
Two legs? I mean, imagine yourself like that.'
The other whinnied, and hoofed the ground,
then began to sing a song, a wrenching lament
for a red-haired woman, that intensified
when the second horse joined in, so the man
slipped away, head down, back to the harbour.

The Heron

PAUL FARLEY

One of the most begrudging avian take-offs
is the heron's *fucking hell, all right, all right,*
I'll go to the garage for your flaming fags
cranky departure, though once they're up
their flight can be extravagant. I watched
one big spender climb the thermal staircase,
a calorific waterspout of frogs
and sticklebacks, the undercarriage down
and trailing. Seen from antiquity
you gain the Icarus thing; seen from my childhood
that cursing man sets out for Superkings,
though the heron cares for neither as it struggles
into its wings then soars sunwards and throws
its huge overcoat across the earth.

Chameleon

HELEN IVORY

My mother kept a chameleon instead of a dog and when I
was at school it did the job of passing notes to my father.
It was very clever at appearing anywhere around the house
– hanging by its tail from the curtain pole, materialising
suddenly from the pattern of the armchair. The quickness
of its eyes meant he never got away, and when its elastic
tongue delivered the message somewhere between temple
and cheek, it would always come with the clatter of pans
from down the hall, or the angry whiz of a blender.

Crustacean Island

KAY RYAN

There could be an island paradise
where crustaceans prevail.
Click, click, go the lobsters
with their china mitts and
articulated tails.
It would not be sad like whales
with their immense and patient sieving
and the sobering modesty
of their general way of living.
It would be an island blessed
with only cold-blooded residents
and no human angle.
It would echo with a thousand castanets
and no flamencos.

Home Truths

JOHN WHITWORTH

Firm friends foster no wishlists.
Fire dogs gladden no brasses.
Frock coats flatter no waistlines.
Fly guys batter no punchbags.
Fish eyes slubber no fleabites.
Flesh pots gladden no phantoms.
French fries coarsen no lampreys.
Feast days plunder no parsleys.
Fruit bats clatter no cornstalks.
Fresh gourds threaten no porkers.
Flash girls butter no foreskins.
Fire trucks hasten no lightships.
Flown birds twitter no courtships.
Fox turds gather no mothballs.
Foul curds fatten no hedgehogs.
Flush nerds buckle no hairshirts.
Fat worms bubble no sheepdips.
Fur balls button no fatlips.
False beards beckon no hairclips.
Farm carts clutter no coalpits.
File cards foster no cock-ups.
Fine folks favour no pisspots.
Fine wines pleasure no penguins.
Fine words butter no parsnips.

A Few
Precepts

OLI HAZZARD

Always keep the end in mind.
Don't blow your brains too soon.
Premature enunciation leads to stress
for the foetus in the womb.
Mend their ways. Part what you see.
Remember: what some people call a marriage bed
some people call a tomb.
Potato potato. Pronounce scone as scone.
Pronounce grass as grass. Bastard is
as bastard does. Keep your mind
on a short leash. Don't let it eat from
the table. If it barks at you,
bark back. Lock it in a room.
If it needs to relieve itself, never put paper down.
Soon enough it'll be line-broken.
Pick up after it. Be prepared to eat shit
sandwiches. That picnic
will be no picnic. Sew someone else's name
in your pants. Make sure your friends are freedom-
range. Beware your uniform.
do not let it beware you. Drop twenty
and give yourself twenty.
Forget how many necks these woods have grown.
Only loot what you can't afford. Don't touch
yourself. Don't let your moods
get in a room together. Chew the fat
ones, then spit them out.
Drink sake for the sake
of a joke. Give your children only middle names.

If you remember nothing, you've had a good time.
If you pick at that thread
you'll be caught with your pants down.
By the time you're done, home will be the place where,
when you have to go there,
they have to report you to the relevant authorities.

Proverbial Ballade

WENDY COPE

Fine words won't turn the icing pink;
A wild rose has no employees;
Who boils his socks will make them shrink;
Who catches cold is sure to sneeze.
Who has two legs must wash two knees;
Who breaks the egg will find the yolk;
Who locks his door will need his keys –
So say I and so say the folk.

You can't shave with a tiddlywink,
Nor make red wine from garden peas,
Nor show a blindworm how to blink,
Nor teach an old racoon Chinese.
The juiciest orange feels the squeeze;
Who spends his portion will be broke;
Who has no milk can make no cheese –
So say I and so say the folk.

He makes no blot who has no ink,
Nor gathers honey who keeps no bees.
The ship that does not float will sink;
Who'd travel far must cross the seas.
Lone wolves are seldom seen in threes;
A conker ne'er becomes an oak;
Rome wasn't built by chimpanzees –
So say I and so say the folk.

Envoi

Dear friends! If adages like these
Should seem banal, or just a joke,
Remember fish don't grow on trees –
So say I and so say the folk.

Like the Proverbial

JOHN WHITWORTH

I'm drinking my drink at the last chance saloon.
I'm over the limit and over the moon.
Though I've gone on the town, to the dogs, to the bad,
Still I'm one of the boys and a bit of a lad.

Do you know where I'm coming from, know where I'm at?
When they're moving the goalposts I keep a straight bat.
In a game of two halves, I keep serving straight aces
To get a result on a regular basis.

It's been dubbed a sea-change and the tide's on the turn.
Now it's money for jam and there's money to burn.
But you haven't a prayer if you haven't the clout
And the word on the streets is THE JURY IS OUT.

There's a confidence nosedive, an upsurge in crime,
Still I'm going for broke now, at this point in time.
Far too many loose cannon just shoot from the hip,
And firm hands on the tiller must steady the ship.

With the dollar in free fall, the markets are nervous.
The eyes of the world are all paying lip service.
They claim heads will roll if we sit on our hands.
We must change hearts and minds and repackage our brands.

Community leaders, the movers and shakers,
Power-brokers, risk-takers, butt-kickers, ball-breakers,
Have taken down barriers, mended their fences.
Come out with one voice and by general consensus.

Put your ears to the ground in your ivory towers,
You must vest the grass roots with executive powers,
Out there in the real world the silent majority
Speak for the people with growing authority.

You must kick that in touch. You must take this on board.
You must hit the right note, ring a bell, strike a chord.
You can stink like a polecat or smell like a rose is,
You're out of your SKULL and you get up our noses!

Too gutted and knackered to put in the boot,
I'm as drunk as a skunk, I'm as pissed as a newt,
I'm as sick as a parrot, as sick as a dog.
I'll go out like a light and I'll sleep like a log.

Symposium

PAUL MULDOON

You can lead a horse to water but you can't make it hold
its nose to the grindstone and hunt with the hounds.
Every dog has a stitch in time. Two heads? You've been sold
one good turn. One good turn deserves a bird in the hand.

A bird in the hand is better than no bread.
To have your cake is to pay Paul.
Make hay while you can still hit the nail on the head.
For want of a nail the sky might fall.

People in glass houses can't see the wood
for the new broom. Rome wasn't built between two stools.
Empty vessels wait for no man.

A hair of the dog is a friend indeed.
There's no fool like the fool
who's shot his bolt. There's no smoke after the horse is gone.

Nothing's As It Should Be

ROBERT PHILLIPS

The pie is not easy.
The pin is not neat.
The bees are not busy.
The milk is not meek.

The hound, not lazy.
The clams aren't happy.
The loon is not crazy.
The friend-in-need, snappish.

The cat piss is not mean.
The thieves are not thick.
The hound's tooth is not clean.
The winks are not quick.

The fiddle is not fit.
The bells, never clear.
The honey's never sweet.
The three-dollar bill, unqueer.

The molasses isn't slow.
The church mouse, not poor.
The mule, not stubborn in toto.
The ceiling's not another's floor.

The bunny isn't dumb.
The toothache doesn't hurt.
The rail is not thinsome.
The soil's not cheap as dirt.

The grass isn't green.
The horses aren't healthy.
Nothing's right about the rain:
God's not in Heaven, all's not OK.

With Hindsight

The way to the stomach is through the heart.
If he's been eating with his eyes, ask him exactly how much
He's been beholding. If his words are drowned out
By his actions, tell him not to protest so much.

OLI HAZZARD

A little yearning is a dangerous thing; he clearly hasn't been
Eating his apple-a-day. If only the incision were skin-deep.
No wonder he's blind. But even a worm will turn –
Softly, softly – from a piece of string to a length of old rope.

Give him enough and he'll hang.
If God had meant us to fall, he'd have given us wings –
But then there'd be no work for drinkers.
So, those who cannot preach, practise.
Truth is wasted on the tongue.

Adage

BILLY COLLINS

When it's late at night and branches
Are banging against the windows,
you might think that love is just a matter

of leaping out of the frying pan of yourself
into the fire of someone else,
but it's a little more complicated than that.

It's more like trading the two birds
who might be hiding in that bush
for the one you are not holding in your hand.

A wise man once said that love
was like forcing a horse to drink
but then everyone stopped thinking of him as wise.

Let us be clear about something.
Love is not as simple as getting up
on the wrong side of the bed wearing the emperor's clothes.

No, it's more like the way the pen
feels after it has defeated the sword.
It's a little like the penny saved or the nine dropped stitches.

You look at me through the halo of the last candle
and tell me love is an ill wind
that has no turning, a road that blows no good,

but I am here to remind you,
as our shadows tremble on the walls,
that love is the early bird who is better late than never.

Ivory

SIMON ARMITAGE

No more mularkey,
no baloney. No more cuffuffle
or shenanigans;

all that caboodle
is niet dobra. It will end
this minute.

No more fuss
or palaver; no more mush
or blarney. No flowers,

by request; no offence meant,
and none taken. No more blab,
none of that ragtag

and bobtail business,
or ballyhoo or
balderdash

and no jackassery, or flannel,
or galumphing.
Listen:

from this point forward
it's ninety-nine
and forty-four hundredths

per cent pure.
And no remarks
from the peanut gallery.

Speech balloon

IMTIAZ DHARKER

The Liverpool boss was pretty chuffed with himself,
said the news report, for being so tough
when he decided to snub the obvious choice
and go instead for the goal machine.
I'm over the moon, they said he said.
I'm over the moon, he said.

The Barnsley manager was lost for words
to describe his feelings when Chelsea fell
to the Tykes. *We played fantastic.*
I never thought we'd do it again
but we did, we did, and all I can say is
I'm over the moon, they said he said.
I'm over the moon, he said.

The Hollywood mum was way beyond thrilled
according to friends, when she delivered
into the world, not one bouncing baby
but twins instead to the astonished dad.
I'm over the moon, they said she said.
I'm over the moon, she said.

Bollywood's hottest couple was proud to be blessed
by the jubilant father, the superstar.
It's a match made in heaven, he said to the press,
Between two shooting stars with shining careers
and I'm over the moon, of course, he said.
I'm over the moon, he said.

The Malaysian nation went mad with joy
on independence day in its fiftieth year
when a doctor-cum-part-time-model,
a local boy, went up into space in a Russian Soyuz
and in zero gravity, performed his *namaaz*.
All of Malaysia over the moon, they said on the news,
twenty-seven million people over the moon.

You must have noticed, it's really quite clear,
this condition has spread, it's happening there,
it's happening here. It's full-blown, grown
beyond every border, to the furthest corner
of every country where English is spoken
or English is known.

There's no one just satisfied or mildly pleased
or chipper or chirpy, contented or cheerful,
no one glad or gratified, delighted or jubilant,
elated, ecstatic, joyful or gleeful.
All the happy people have left this world.
You won't come across them any time soon

and if it's happy sound-bites you're looking for
you need to look way over your head
for the words in balloons

to the place where the cow keeps jumping
over and over
with all the footballers, team managers

and lottery winners, world superstars,
heroes and champions and legends and lovers
and proud mums and dads

and the whole of Malaysia

over the moon
over the moon
over the over the over the moon.

What She Said

BILLY COLLINS

When he told me he expected me to pay for dinner,
I was like give me a break.

I was not the exact equivalent of give me a break.
I was just similar to give me a break.

As I said, I was like give me a break.

I would love to tell you
how I was able to resemble give me a break
without actually being identical to give me a break,

but all I can say is that I sensed
a similarity between me and give me a break.

And that was close enough
at that point in the evening

even if it meant I would fall short
of standing up from the table and screaming
give me a break,

for God's sake will you please give me a break?!

No, for that moment
with the rain streaking the restaurant windows
and the waiter approaching,

I felt the most I could be was like

to a certain degree

give me a break.

Oh, My God!

BILLY COLLINS

Not only in church
and nightly by their bedsides
do young girls pray these days.

Wherever they go,
prayer is woven into their talk
like a bright thread of awe.

Even at the pedestrian mall
outbursts of praise
spring unbidden from their glossy lips.

Ode to American English

BARBARA HAMBY

I was missing English one day, American, really,
    with its pill-popping Hungarian goulash of everything
from Anglo-Saxon to Zulu, because British English
    is not the same, if the paperback dictionary
I bought at Brentano's on the Avenue de l'Opera
    is any indication, too cultured by half. Oh, the English
know their dahlias, but what about doowop, donuts,
    Dick Tracy, Tricky Dick? With their elegant Oxfordian
accents, how could they understand my yearning for the hotrod,
    hotdog, hot flash vocabulary of the U. S. of A.,
the fragmented fandango of Dagwood's everyday flattening
    of Mr Beasley on the sidewalk, fetuses floating
on billboards, drive-by monster hip-hop stereos shaking
    the windows of my dining room like a 7.5 earthquake,
Ebonics, Spanglish, 'you know' used as comma and period,
    the inability of 90% of the population to get the present perfect:
I have went, I have saw, I have tooken Jesus into my heart,
    the battle cry of the Bible Belt, but no one uses
the King James anymore, only plain-speak versions,
    in which Jesus, raising Lazarus from the dead, says,
'Dude, wake up,' and the L-man bolts up like a B-movie
    mummy, 'Whoa, I was toasted.' Yes, ma'am,
I miss the mongrel plentitude of American English, its fall-guy,
    rat-terrier, dog-pound neologisms, the bomb of it all,
the rushing River Jordan backwoods mutability of it, the low-rider,
    boom-box cruise of it, from New Joisey to Ha-wah-ya
with its sly dog, malasada-scarfing beach blanket lingo
    to the ubiquitous Valley Girl's *like-like* stuttering,

shopaholic rant. I miss its quotidian beauty, its querulous
  back-biting righteous indignation, its preening rotgut
flag-waving cowardice. *Suffering Succotash*, sputters
  Sylvester the Cat; *sine die*, say the pork-bellied legislators
of the swamps and plains. I miss all those guys, their Tweety-bird
  resilience, their Doris Day optimism, the candid unguent
of utter unhappiness on every channel, the midnight televangelist
  euphoric stew, the junk mail, voice mail vernacular.
On every boulevard and rue I miss the Tarzan cry of Johnny
  Weissmuller, Johnny Cash, Johnny B. Goode,
and all the smart-talking, gum-snapping hard-girl dialogue,
  finger-popping x-rated street talk, sports babble,
Cheetoes, Cheerios, chili dog diatribes. Yeah, I miss them all,
  sitting here on my sidewalk throne sipping champagne
verses lined up like hearses, metaphors juking, nouns zipping
  in my head like Corvettes on Dexadrine, French verbs
slitting my throat, yearning for James Dean to jump my curb.

I swear

IMTIAZ DHARKER

Because I turned up from Bombay
too prissy to be rude
because you arrived via Leeds and Burnley
you thought it would do me good

to learn some Language. So

you never just fell, you went arse over tits,
and you were never not bothered
you just couldn't be arsed, and when
you laughed you laughed like an effing drain
and when there was pain it was a pain
in the arse.

That was just the start: you taught me
all the Language you knew
right through the alphabet from a to z,
from first to last, from bad to worse and worser
and the very worst you could muster.

I learned the curses. I learned the curser.
So proper you looked in your nice shoes and suit
until you produced Language like magic
out of your mouth and I was impressed

and oh I fell for you arse over tits
and when I said so you laughed like a drain
and we blinded and swore like the daft buggers

we were, all the way down Clerkenwell
and all the way up on the train
to the Horseshoe Pass.

And I tell you, since you went it's a pain
in the arse, and when some days I feel like shit
or when I say that I feel flat, I swear
I hear you laugh like a drain.
Not just flat, Mrs, Flat as a witch's tit,
that's what you say. Flat

as a witch's tit.

Invective

THOMAS LUX

Boils, pocks, and blood blisters, I pray you suffer them,
your goat grow fevered
and leak the yellow milk, I pray moles claw holes
in your head, stones be always in your shoe, fire
in your neck, slop in your cooking pot.
I pray there be rubber bullets in your gun,
I pray your daughter marry for love,
I pray your son wish to be a poet.
I pray your mother take a young lover in front of your father,
I pray it be revealed you keep your toothpicks in your beard,
I pray you be turned down
if you register to vote, I pray your wife fucks you
in the ass, I pray all your lug-nut-dumb offscourings
disdain you, I pray your next breath,
and each one thereafter, fills your lungs
with the stink of your corpse.

A Malediction

PETER DIDSBURY

Spawn of a profligate hog.
May the hand of your self-abuse
be afflicted by a palsy.
May an Order in Council
deprive you of a testicle.
May your teeth be rubbed with turds
by a faceless thing from Grimsby.
May your past begin to remind you
of an ancient butter paper
found lying behind a fridge.
May the evil odour of an elderly male camel
fed since birth on buckets of egg mayonnaise
enter your garden and shrivel up all your plants.
May all reflective surfaces
henceforth teach you to shudder.
And may you thus be deprived
of the pleasures of walking by water.
And may you grow even fatter.
And may you, moreover, develop athlete's foot.
May your friends cease to excuse you,
your wife augment the thicket of horns on your brow,
and even your enemies weary of malediction.
May your girth already gross
embark on a final exponential increase.
And at the last may your body, in bursting,
make your name live for ever,
an unparalleled warning to children.

Rather

THOMAS LUX

Rather strapped face to face with a corpse, rather an asp
forced down my throat, rather a glass
tube inserted in my urethra
and then member smashed
with a hammer, rather wander the malls of America shopping
for shoes, rather
be lunch, from the ankles down,
for a fish, rather mistake rabbit drops
for capers, or pearls, rather my father's bones crushed to dust
and blown – blinding me – in my eyes,
rather a flash flood of liquid mud,
boulders, branches, drowned dogs, tear through Boys Town
and grind up a thousand orphans, rather
finger puppets
with ice picks
probe me, rather numbness, rather Malaysian tongue worm, rather rue,
rather a starved rat
tied by his tail to my last tooth,
rather memory become mush,
rather no more books be written but on the sole subject of self, rather
a retinal tattoo, rather buckets of bad bacilli and nothing else
to drink, rather the blather
at an English Department meeting, rather
a mountain fall on my head than this,
what I put down here, rather
all of the above than this, this:_____.

One Size Fits All: A Critical Essay

DAVID LEHMAN

Though
Already
Perhaps
However.

On one level,
Among other things,
With
And with.
In a similar vein
To be sure:
Make no mistake.
Nary a trace.

However,
Aside from
With
And with,
Not
And not,
Rather
Manifestly
Indeed.

Which is to say,
In fictional terms,
For reasons that are never made clear,
Not without meaning,
Though (as is far from unusual)
Perhaps too late.

The first thing that must be said is
Perhaps, because
And, not least of all,
Certainly more,
Which is to say
In every other respect
Meanwhile.

But then perhaps
Though
And though
On the whole
Alas.

Moreover
In contrast
And even
Admittedly
Partly because
And partly because
Yet it must be said.

Even more significantly, perhaps
In other words
With
And with,
Whichever way
One thing is clear
Beyond the shadow of a doubt.

The Critic

WILLIAM GRONO

My slow stepfather
boorish and ignorant,
used (often) to say:
'What's a bloody uni student
know about life? Eh? Nothing!
Absolutely fucking nothing! And
I'll tell you something else,
you bloody little pisswit,
you never bloody will either.'

How does one cope with crudity?
I realised of course
that reasoning was useless, yet
I could not help but point out
that understanding did not necessarily
accompany experience; indeed
one could say (I would say)
that one could as it were achieve
a greater a more viable
understanding of life by discussing it
in a spirit of rational disinterest – But
he would always interrupt: 'Ah, shit!'
and stagger off to get another bottle.

He died of course drunk
whilst swimming with a Mrs Montgomery
in the surf below the Ocean View Hotel
at one o'clock in the morning.

He was sixty-seven, penniless,
and probably tubercular.

I, on the other hand
am now an assistant professor
of English literature, and
a not insignificant critic.

Water under the Bridge

KAY RYAN

That's water under
the bridge, we say
siding with the bridge
and no wonder,
given the sloping ways
of water which
grows so grey
and oily, toiling
slowly downward,
its wide dented
slide ever onward;
we aren't demented.

Errata

PAUL MULDOON

For 'Antrim' read 'Armagh'.
For 'mother' read 'other'.
For 'harm' read 'farm'.
For 'feather' read 'father'.

For 'Moncrieff read 'Monteith'.
For '*Béal Fierste*' read '*Béal Feirste*'.
For 'brave' read 'grave'.
For 'revered' read 'reversed'.

For 'married' read 'marred'.
For 'pull' read 'pall'.
For 'ban' read 'bar'.
For 'smell' read 'small'.

For 'spike' read 'spoke'.
For 'lost' read 'last'.
For 'Steinbeck' read 'Steenbeck'.
For 'ludic' read 'lucid'.

For 'religion' read 'region'.
For 'ode' read 'code'.
For 'Jane' read 'Jean'.
For 'rod' read 'road'.

For 'pharoah' read 'pharaoh'.
For '*Fíor-Gael*' read '*Fíor-Ghael*'
For 'Jeffrey' read 'Jeffery'.
For 'vigil' read 'Virgil'.

For 'flageolet' read 'fava'.
For 'veto' read 'vote'.
For 'Aiofe' read 'Aoife'.
For 'anecdote' read 'antidote'.

For 'Rosemont' read 'Mount Rose'.
For 'plump' read 'plumb'.
For 'hearse' read 'hears'.
For 'loom' read 'bloom'.

Eirata

(after Muldoon)

IGGY McGOVERN

For 'Armagh' read 'Armani'
For 'brat' read 'Brut'
For 'Carmelite' read 'Camel Light'
For Dáil' read 'doll'
For 'exiles' read 'X-Files'
For 'faction' read 'fiction'
For 'gael' read 'gaol'
For 'hallowed' read 'hollowed'
For 'island' read 'inland'
For 'jarvey' read 'Charvet'
For 'Kerry' read 'curry'
For 'Ludo' read 'Lotto'
For 'morals' read 'morels'
For 'novena' read 'novella'
For 'Ogra' read 'Oprah'
For 'parish' read 'perish'
For 'Quoof' read 'quiff'
For 'rosary' read 'Rotary'
For 'sacred' read 'scared'
For 'traitor' read 'trattoria'
For 'Ulster' read 'Hustler'
For 'virtuous' read 'virtual'
For 'widows' read 'Windows'
For 'X-cert' read 'excerpt'
For 'yawp' read 'yob'
For 'zed' read 'zee'

Acknowledgements

The poems in this anthology are reprinted from the following books, all by permission of the publishers listed unless stated otherwise. Thanks are due to all the copyright holders cited below for their kind permission:

Fleur Adcock: 'Smokers for Celibacy' from *Poems 1960-2000* (Bloodaxe Books, 2000). **Kim Addonizio**: 'You Don't Know What Love Is' from *What Is This Thing Called Love* (W.W. Norton & Company, US, 2004) and *Wild Nights: New & Selected Poems* (Bloodaxe Books, UK, 2015). **John Agard**: 'Alternative Anthem' from *Alternative Anthem: Selected Poems* (Bloodaxe Books, 2012). **Simon Armitage**: 'Ivory' from *Zoom!* (Bloodaxe Books, 1989). **Tiffany Atkinson**: 'The Man Whose Left Hand Thought It Was a Chicken', from *Kink and Particle* (Seren Books, 2006).

Connie Bensley: 'Choice' from *Finding a Leg to Stand On: New & Selected Poems* (Bloodaxe Books, 2012). **Caroline Bird**: 'I Know This Because You Told Me' from *Looking Through Letterboxes* (Carcanet Press, 2002); 'Trouble Came to the Turnip from Trouble' from *Trouble Came to the Turnip* (Carcanet Press, 2006). **Eleanor Brown**: 'Bitcherel' from *Maiden Speech* (Bloodaxe Books, 1996).

Lucille Clifton: 'homage to my hips' from *Good Woman: Poems and a Memoir 1969-1980* (BOA Editions, 1987). **Billy Collins**: 'Forgetfulness' from *Taking Off Emily Dickinson's Clothes: Selected Poems* (Picador, 2000); 'Adage' and 'Oh, My God!' from *Ballistics* (Picador, 2008); 'What She Said' from *Horoscopes for the Dead* (Picador, 2011); all by permission of Macmillan Publishers Ltd. **Wendy Cope**: 'Proverbial Ballade' from *Two Cures for Love: Selected Poems 1979-2006* (Faber & Faber, 2008); 'My Funeral' from *Family Values* (Faber & Faber, 2011). **Ivor Cutler**: 'For sixpence' from *Many Flies Have Feathers* (Trigram Press, 1973); 'Three Sisters' from *A Flat Man* (Trigram Press, 1977); both by permission of the Literary Estate of Ivor Cutler.

Julia Darling: 'Forecasting' from The Poetry Virgins: *Sauce* (Bloodaxe Books/Diamond Twig Press, 1994), by permission of the author's family. **Imtiaz Dharker:** 'Speech balloon' and 'I swear' from *Over the Moon* (Bloodaxe Books, 2014). *Peter Didsbury:* 'Malediction' from *Scenes from a Long Sleep: New & Collected Poems* (Bloodaxe Books, 2003). **Stephen Dobyns:** 'Spiritual Chickens' from *Velocities: New & Selected Poems* (Penguin Books, USA, 1994; Bloodaxe Books, UK, 1996). **Finuala Dowling:** 'Well' and 'Doo-wop girls of the universe' from *Doo-Wop Girls of the Universe* (Penguin Books, South Africa, 2006); 'How Sweet the Dead Are Now' from *Change Is Possible* (The Poetry Trust, Aldeburgh, 2014), by permission of Blake Friedman Literary, Film & TV Agency. **Paul Durcan:** 'Tullynoe: Tête-à-Tête in the Priest's Parlour' from *A Snail in My Prime: New & Selected Poems* (The Harvill Press, 1993); 'A Man Besotted by his Batch' from *Praise in Which I Live and Move and Have My Being* (Harvill Secker, 2012).

Russell Edson: 'Counting Sheep' from *The Tunnel: Selected Poems* (Oberlin College Press, 1994); 'The Antiques Shop' and 'The Joy Attendant on the Little Journey' from *The Tormented Mirror* (University of Pittsburgh Press, 2001). **Jonathan Edwards:** 'The Voice in which My Mother Read to Me' from *My Family and Other Superheroes* (Seren Books, 2014). **Martín Espada:** 'DSS Dream' from *Alabanza: New and Selected Poems 1982-2002* (W.W. Norton & Company, 2003).

U.A. Fanthorpe: 'You Will Be Hearing from Us Shortly' from *New & Collected Poems* (Enitharmon Press, 2010). **Paul Farley:** 'The Heron' from *Tramp in Flames* (Picador, 2006), by permission of Macmillan Publishers Ltd. **Gus Ferguson:** 'The Metempsychosis of the Yak' from *Light Verse at the End of the Tunnel* (David Philip Publishers, Cape Town, 1996), 'Not a rumour, a murmur' from *Dubious delights: of ageing and other follies* (Unpublished Manuscript Press, Cape Town, 2006); 'Samsara' from *Holding Pattern* (Quartz Press, Parkhurst, South Africa, 2009); all by permission of the author. **Peter Finch:** 'Kipper on the Lips' from *Selected Later Poems* (Seren Books, 2007). **Duncan Forbes:** 'America' and 'Job Description' from *Voice Mail* (Enitharmon Press, 2002). **Kate Fox:** 'Our Ends in the North' from *Fox Populi* (Smokestack Books, 2013).

John Gallas: 'For this Islamic enthusiasm, on the other hand, (William) Whiston was expelled from Cambridge in 1709' from *Forty Lies* (Carcanet

Press, 2010). **Deborah Garrison:** 'Fight Song' from *A Working Girl Can't Win* (Random House, NY, 1998). **William Grono:** 'The Critic' from *On the Edge* (Freshwater Bay Press, Australia, 1980).

Barbara Hamby: 'Ode to American English' from *Babel* (University of Pittsburgh Press, 2004). **Sophie Hannah:** 'Rubbish at Adultery' from *Pessimism for Beginners* (Carcanet Press, 2007). **Matt Harvey:** 'Thwok', Wimbledon Championships 2010 Poet commission, *Mindless Body Spineless Mind* (Man in the Quote, 2012), by permission of the author. **Geoff Hattersley:** 'How She Puts It' and 'In Phil's Butchers' from *Back of Beyond: New & Selected Poems* (Smith/Doorstop Books, 2006). **Oli Hazzard:** 'A Few Precepts', 'With Hindsight' and 'The Inability to Recall the Precise Word for Something' from *Between Two Windows* (Carcanet Press, 2012). **Dermot Healy:** 'One Minute with Eileen' from *The Reed Bed* (Gallery Press, 2001) by permission of The Gallery Press, Loughcrew, Oldcastle, Co. Meath, Ireland. **John Hegley:** 'A Declaration of Need' from *New & Selected Potatoes* (Bloodaxe Books, 2013) and *Beyond Our Kennel* (Methuen, 1998), by permission of Methuen. **W.N. Herbert:** 'The Big Wet' and 'To a Mousse' from *The Laurelude* (Blood-axe Books, 1998). **Rita Ann Higgins:** 'The Did-You-Come-Yets of the Western World' and 'Woman's Inhumanity to Woman' from *Throw in the Vowels: New & Selected Poems* (Bloodaxe Books, 2005). **Selima Hill:** 'Cow' and 'Please Can I Have a Man' from *Gloria: Selected Poems* (Blood-axe Books, 2008). **Tony Hoagland:** 'Romantic Moment' and 'My Father's Vocabulary' from *Unincorporated Persons in the Late Honda Dynasty* (Gray-wolf Press, USA; Bloodaxe Books, UK, 2010), by permission of Gray-wolf Press, www.graywolfpress.org.

Helen Ivory: 'Chameleon' from *Waiting for Bluebeard* (Bloodaxe Books, 2014)

Jackie Kay: 'Maw Broon Goes for Colonic Irrigation' from *New Poems Chiefly in the Scottish Dialect*, ed. Robert Crawford (Polygon, 2009), by permission of the author. **Brendan Kennelly:** 'Front Gate' from *Poetry My Arse* (Bloodaxe Books, 1995).

Frank Kuppner: 'A Prodigy of Nature' from *A God's Breakfast* (Carcanet Press, 2004). **David Lehman:** 'One Size Fits All: A Critical

Essay' from *New and Selected Poems* (Scribner, 2013). **Michael Leunig:** 'The Awfulisers' from *A Bunch of Poesy* (Angus & Robertson, Sydney, 1992), first published in *The Age* newspaper, 14 September 1991, by permission of the author. **Joanne Limburg:** 'Inner Bloke' from *Femenismo* (Bloodaxe Books, 2000). **Liz Lochhead:** 'The Man in the Comic Strip' from *A Choosing: Selected Poems* (Polygon/Birlinn, 2011). **Thomas Lux:** 'The People of the Other Village' from *Split Horizon* (Houghton Mifflin, USA, 1994); 'Plague Victims Catapulted Over Walls into Besieged City' from *The Street of Clocks* (Houghton Mifflin, USA, 2001); 'Rather' from *The Cradle Place* (Houghton Mifflin, USA, 2004); 'Invective' from *God Particles* (Houghton Mifflin, 2008); all from *Selected Poems* (Bloodaxe Books, UK, 2014).

Roger McGough: 'Let Me Die a Youngman's Death' from *Collected Poems* (Viking/ Penguin Books, 2007), by permission of Peters Fraser & Dunlop; 'Not for Me a Youngman's Death' from *As Far As I Know* (Penguin Books, 2012), by permission of United Agents. **Iggy McGovern:** 'Errata' from *The King of Suburbia* (Dedalus Press, 2005). **Ian McMillan:** 'Pit Closure as Art' and 'Burst Pipe with "A Level" Notes' from *Dad, the Donkey's on Fire* (Carcanet Press, 1994). **Bill Manhire:** 'Hotel Emergencies' from *Selected Poems* (Carcanet Press, 2014). **Lorraine Mariner:** 'Stanley' from *Furniture* (Picador, 2009), by permission of Macmillan Publishers Ltd. **Glyn Maxwell:** 'Don't Waste Your Breath' from *The Boys at Twilight: Poems 1990-1995* (Bloodaxe Books, 2000). **Irfan Merchant:** 'Address Tae Chicken Tikka Masala' from *Out of Bounds: British Black & Asian Poets*, ed. Jackie Kay, James Procter & Gemma Robinson (Blood-axe Books, 2012), by permission of the author. **Adrian Mitchell:** 'Ten Ways to Avoid Lending Your Wheelbarrow to Anybody' and 'Shaven Heads' from *Come On Everybody: Poems 1953-2008* (Bloodaxe Books, 2012). **Paul Muldoon:** 'Errata' and 'Symposium' from *Hay* (Faber & Faber, 1998).

Daljit Nagra: 'Singh Song!' from *Look We Have Coming to Dover!* (Faber & Faber, 2007).

Gregory O'Brien: 'Love Poem' from *Beauties of the Octagonal Pool* (Auckland University Press, 2012), by permission of the author and the publisher. **Julie O'Callaghan:** 'Managing the Common Herd' and 'The

Sounds of Earth' from *Tell Me This Is Normal: New & Selected Poems* (Bloodaxe Books, 2008). **Sharon Olds:** 'Self-portrait, Rear View' from *One Secret Thing* (Jonathan Cape, 2009), by permission of the Random House Group Ltd.

Robert Phillips: 'Nothing's As It Should Be', first published in *Chautauqua Literary Journal, 2* (2005), by permission of the author.

Simon Rae: 'Nursery Rhyme' from *Soft Targets* (Bloodaxe Books, 1991). **Peter Reading:** extract from *Going On* (1985), 'This is unclean ...', from *Collected Poems 2: Poems 1985-1996* (Bloodaxe Books, 1996). **Deryn Rees-Jones:** 'Sheep Piece' from *Signs Around a Dead Body* (Seren Books, 1998). **Sam Riviere:** 'The Prince' from *81 Austerities* (Faber & Faber, 2012). **Michael Rosen:** 'I ran away from home', from *In the Colonie* (Penguin Books, 2005). **Kay Ryan:** 'Crustacean Island', 'Blandeur', 'Spiderweb' and 'Water under the Bridge' from *Odd Blocks: Selected and New Poems* (Carcanet Press, 2011).

Jo Shapcott: 'Lies', 'Love Song with a Flock of Sheep' and 'Goat' from *Her Book: Poems 1988-98* (Faber & Faber, 2006). **Ken Smith:** 'The Chicken Variations' from *Shed: Poems 1980-2001* (Bloodaxe Books, 2002). **Marin Sorescu:** 'Superstition' and 'Omens' from *Selected Poems*, tr. Michael Hamburger (Bloodaxe Books, 1983). **Matthew Sweeney:** 'Black Moon' from *Black Moon* (Jonathan Cape, 2007), by permission of the Random House Group Ltd; 'Horse Music' from *Horse Music* (Bloodaxe Books, 2013).

James Tate: 'It Happens Like This', 'How the Pope Is Chosen', 'The Ice Cream Man' and 'The Native Americans' from *The Eternal Ones of the Dream: Selected Poems 1990-2010* (Ecco Press/HarperCollins, 2012). **Elizabeth Thomas:** 'Lies My Mother Told Me' from *From the Front of the Classroom* (Antrim House, 2008).

Priscila Uppal: 'The Old Debate of Don Quixote vs Sancho Panza' from *Successful Tragedies: Poems 1998-2010* (Bloodaxe Books, 2010).

Lorna Wallace: 'Tae a Selfie', from http://lornalouwriting.wordpress.com, by permission of the author. **Matthew Welton:** 'The fundament of wonderment' from *The Book of Matthew* (Carcanet Press, 2003). **John Whitworth:** 'Home Truths', 'From My Rough Goatbook' and 'Like the

Proverbial' from *The Whitworth Gun* (Peterloo Poets, 2002), by permission of the author; 'Ruling-Class Sonnets with Capitals and Obscenities' from *Girlie Gangs* (Enitharmon Press, 2012). **Chrissy Williams**: 'Sheep' from *The Best British Poetry 2011*, ed. Roddy Lumsden (Salt Publishing, 2011), by permission of the author. **John Hartley Williams**: 'The Good Ship Venus' from *Canada* (Bloodaxe Books, 1997), by permission of the author's estate. **Kit Wright**: 'Everyone Hates the English' and 'The All Purpose Country and Western Self-Pity Song' from *Hoping It Might Be So: Poems 1974-2000* (Leviathan, 2000; Faber Finds, 2008), by permission of the author.

Dean Young: 'Convinced by a Nalungiaq Song' from *Ready-Made Bouquet* (Stride, 2005), by permission of the author; 'I See a Lily on Thy Brow' and 'Static City' from *Bender: New & Selected Poems* (Copper Canyon Press, 2012).

Benjamin Zephaniah: 'This Be The Worst' from *Propa Propaganda* (Bloodaxe Books, 2001).

Every effort has been made to trace copyright holders of the poems published in this book. The editor and publisher apologise if any material has been included without permission or without the appropriate acknowledgement, and would be glad to be told of anyone who has not been consulted.

Index of poets